# Data Structures and Algorithms Using C

**T. Primya,**

Assistant Professor, Department of Computer Science and Engineering,

Dr.N.G.P. Institute of Technology, Coimbatore.

**G. Kanagaraj,**

Assistant Professor, Department of Computer Science and Engineering,

Kumaraguru College of Technology, Coimbatore.

**T. Sudhakar,**

Assistant Professor, Department of Computer Technology,

Anna University MIT Campus, Chennai.


**Published by**

**Data Structures and Algorithms Using C**



ISBN 978-93-86176-73-8

**Authors**

T. Primya

G. Kanagaraj

T. Sudhakar

**Bonfring**

309, 2nd Floor, 5th Street Extension, Gandhipuram,

Coimbatore-641 012.

Tamilnadu, India.

E-mail: info@bonfring.org

Website: www.bonfring.org

Phone: 0422 4213231

# Dedicated to

*Our Lovable Son K. Rithvik*

**T. Primya & G. Kanagaraj**

*To my son S. Amudhan and my wife R. Sudha*

**T. Sudhakar**

# Preface

The goal of the textbook "Data Structures and Algorithms using C" help you to understand different concepts of data structures. We also tried to present topics that discuss the theoretical basics of data structures and also its applied aspects.

The brief content of the book is as follows:

Chapter 1 gives the introduction to data structures

Chapter 2 covers the concept of ADT and Linked List

Chapter 3 deals with Stack and Queue ADT

Chapter 4 covers the Tree Data Structures

Chapter 5 tells about Balanced Trees

Chapter 6 deals with Hashing

Chapter 7 covers the different Graph Concepts in Data Structures

Chapter 8 deals with types of sorting

Chapter 9 covers the External Sorting

Chapter 10 is devoted to Searching algorithm

We have written this book out of our interest and have tried my best to make it an interesting reading.

# Acknowledgement

I would first like to thank Almighty, for showering his blessing on me to bring this book a complete one.

I wish to express my profound gratitude to Dr.Nalla G Palaniswami MD., A.B(USA), Chairman of KMCH, Dr.Thavamani D Palaniswami MD.,A.B (USA), Secretary of Dr.N.G.P Institute of Technology, Dr.K. Porkumaran M.E., Ph.D., Principal of Dr.N.G.P Institute of Technology, Dr.S.V. Sudha M.E., Ph.D., Head of the Department, Department of Computer Science and Engineering for their ideal support.

I also wish to express my profound thanks to all those who helped in making this book a reality. Above all I want to thank my husband, G. Kanagaraj, M.E., PhD., who supported and encouraged me in spite of all the time it took me away from them.

Much needed moral support and encouragement is provided on numerous occasions by family and friends. I wish to thank the publisher and the entire team of Bonfring Publication who have taken immense pleasure to craft this book.

| **Chapter** | **Contents** | **Page No** |
|---|---|---|
| **1** | **Data Structure** | **1** |
| | 1.1. Need for Data Structures | 1 |
| | 1.2. Selecting A Data Structure | 1 |
| | 1.3. Types of Data Structures | 1 |
| | 1.4. Overview of Data Structures | 2 |
| **2** | **Abstract Data Types (ADTS)** | **6** |
| | 2.1. ADT Dictionary | 6 |
| | 2.2. The List ADT | 7 |
| | 2.3. Types of Linked List | 8 |
| | 2.4. Singly Linked List: [one-way List] | 9 |
| | 2.5. Doubly Linked Lists | 20 |
| | 2.6. Circular Linked List | 21 |
| | 2.7. Application of Linked List | 23 |
| **3** | **Stack and Queue ADT** | **29** |
| | 3.1. Stack Model | 29 |
| | 3.2. Implementation of Stack Using Array | 29 |
| | 3.3. Implementation of Stack Using Linked List | 34 |
| | 3.4. Application of Stack | 37 |
| | 3.5. Queue Model | 49 |
| | 3.6. Implementation of Queue Using Array: [Linear Queue] | 50 |
| | 3.7. Circular Queue | 54 |
| | 3.8. Implementation of Queue Using Linked List | 56 |
| | 3.9. Double Ended Queue | 59 |
| | 3.10. Priority Queue | 62 |
| **4** | **Trees** | **63** |
| | 4.1. Introduction | 63 |
| | 4.2. Terminology in Trees | 63 |
| | 4.3. Implementation of Trees | 69 |
| | 4.4. Binary Tree | 70 |

| | | |
|---|---|---|
| | 4.5. Types of Binary Tree | 70 |
| | 4.6. Binary Tree Representation | 72 |
| | 4.7. Expression Tree | 73 |
| | 4.8. Binary Search Tree | 78 |
| | 4.9. Threaded Binary Trees | 89 |
| | 4.10. Binary Tree Traversals | 92 |
| | 4.11. Priority Queues (Heaps) | 95 |
| **5** | **Balanced Trees** | **107** |
| | 5.1. AVL Trees | 107 |
| | 5.2. Splay Trees | 119 |
| | 5.3. B-Trees | 125 |
| **6** | **Hashing** | **131** |
| | 6.1. Hash Table | 131 |
| | 6.2. Hash Function | 131 |
| | 6.3. Types of Hash Function | 132 |
| | 6.4. Collision | 133 |
| | 6.5. Collision Resolving Strategies | 134 |
| **7** | **Graphs** | **145** |
| | 7.1. Introduction | 145 |
| | 7.2. Graph Terminology | 145 |
| | 7.3. Representation of Graph | 148 |
| | 7.4. Topological Sort | 149 |
| | 7.5. Shortest Path Algorithm | 151 |
| | 7.6. Minimum Spanning Tree | 155 |
| | 7.7. Graph Traversal | 167 |
| | 7.8. Application of DFS | 174 |
| **8** | **Sorting** | **177** |
| | 8.1. Types of Sorting | 177 |
| | 8.2. Insertion Sort | 179 |
| | 8.3. Shell Sort | 183 |
| | 8.4. Heap Sort | 185 |

| | | |
|---|---|---:|
| | 8.5. Merge Sort | 191 |
| | 8.6. Quick Sort | 194 |
| | 8.7. Selection Sort | 198 |
| **9** | **External Sorting** | **202** |
| | 9.1. The Simple Algorithm (2-way merge) | 202 |
| | 9.2. Multiway Merge: [K way] | 203 |
| | 9.3. Polyphase Merge | 203 |
| | 9.4. Replacement Selection | 204 |
| **10** | **Searching Algorithm** | **206** |
| | 10.1. Linear Search: (Sequential Search) | 206 |
| | 10.2. Binary Search | 207 |
| | **Appendix** | **210** |

# CHAPTER 1

# DATA STRUCTURE

Data Structure is a particular way of organizing data in a computer so that it can be used efficiently. Almost every enterprise application uses various types of data structures in one or the other way.

Data Structures is about rendering data elements in terms of some relationship, for better organization and storage. Data Structures are structures programmed to store ordered data, so that various operations can be performed on it easily.

## 1.1. Need for Data Structures

- Data structures organize data to give more efficient programs.
- More powerful computers encourage more complex applications.
- More complex applications demand more calculations.
- Complex computing tasks are unlike our everyday experience.

## 1.2. Selecting A Data Structure

Select a data structure as follows

- Analyze the problem to determine the resource constraints a solution must meet.
- Determine basic operations that must be supported. Quantify resource constraints for each operation.
- Select the data structure that best meets these requirements.

## 1.3. Types of Data Structures

### 1. According to Nature

- Static data structure is an organization or collection of data in memory that is fixed in size. This results in the maximum size needing to be known in advance, as memory cannot be reallocated at a later point.

  Ex: Array

- Dynamic data structure (DDS) refers to an organization or collection of data in memory that has the flexibility to grow or shrink in size, enabling a programmer to control exactly how much memory is utilized.

  Ex: Linked List

## 2. *According to Occurrence*

- In Linear data structure data is stored in consecutive memory location or sequentially and it has unique predecessor and successor.
  Ex: Array, Linked List, stack.
- Non-linear data structures are arranged dynamically i.e., elements do not form sequence.
  Ex: Trees, Graphs.

## 3. *Primitive and Non-Primitive Data Structures*

- Primitive data structures are data structures that normally are directly operated upon by machine-level instructions are known as primitive data structures.
  Ex: integers, reals, logical data, character data, pointer and reference
- Non-Primitive data structures are more complex data structures. These data structures are derived from the primitive data structures. They stress on formation of sets of homogeneous and heterogeneous data elements.
  Ex: Array, Linked List

## 4. *Homogeneous and Non-Homogeneous Data Structures*

- Homogeneous data structures are those data structures that contain only similar type of data e.g. likes a data structure containing only integer or float values.
  Ex: Array
- Heterogeneous Data Structures are those data structures that contain a variety or dissimilar type of data, for e.g. a data structure that can contain various data of different data types like integer, float and character.
  Ex: Union, Structure.

## 1.4.  Overview of Data Structures

### 1. *Arrays*

Arrays a kind of data structure that can store a fixed-size sequential collection of elements of the same type.

An array has predefined size and elements are referenced by index or subscript.

Syntax: <type specifier> array name [size]

Ex: int a[10];

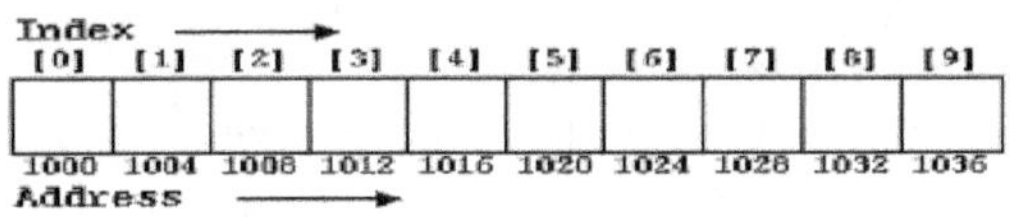



## Advantages

- It is used to represent multiple data items of same type by using only single name.
- It can be used to implement other data structures like linked lists, stacks, queues, trees, graphs etc.
- Searching elements faster as they are stored in continuous memory location.

## Disadvantages

- We must know in advance that how many elements are to be stored in array.
- Array is static structure. It means that array is of fixed size. The memory which is allocated to array cannot be increased or reduced.
- Since array is of fixed size, if we allocate more memory than requirement then the memory space will be wasted. And if we allocate less memory than requirement, then it will create problem.
- The elements of array are stored in consecutive memory locations. So insertions and deletions are very difficult and time consuming.

## 2. Stack

A stack is a linear data structure which is used to store data in a particular order, where insertion and deletion of items takes place at only one end called top of the stack.

It follows Last In First Out(LIFO) order or First In Last Out (FILO) order. Push operation which inserts an element into the stack. Pop operation which removes the last element that was added into the stack. Peep or Peek operation which returns the value of the top the stack.

Ex: Stack of books arranged on a table.

**Stack of books**     **Stack of Coins**     **Memory stack**

### 3. *Queue*

Queue is also an abstract data type or a linear data structure, in which the first element is inserted at one end called REAR (also called tail), and the deletion takes place at other end called as FRONT(also called head).Queue follows First-In-First-Out methodology, i.e., the data item stored first will be accessed first.

Enqueue to insert an item into the queue and Dequeue is used to remove an item from the queue.

Ex: Waiting in a queue to book movie tickets.

### 4. *Linked List*

A linked list is a linear data structure where each element is a separate object. Each element i.e., node of a list is comprising of two items the data field to store values and next filed used to store address of next node and forms a chain. The last node has a reference to null.

### 5. *Tree*

Tree is a widely used abstract data type (ADT) or data structure implementing this ADT that simulates a hierarchical tree structure, with a root value and subtrees of children with a parent node, represented as a set of linked nodes.

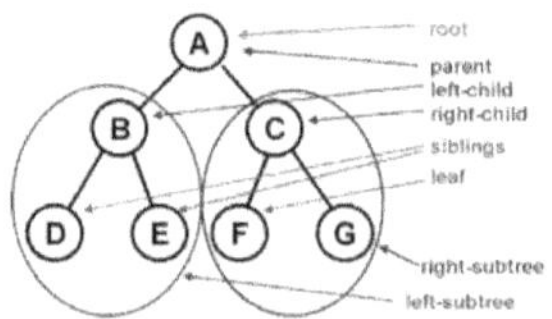


### 6. *Graphs*

A graph data structure consists of a finite set of vertices or nodes or points, together with a set of unordered pairs of these vertices for an undirected graph or a set of ordered pairs for a directed graph.

A G may be defined as a finite set V of vertices and a set E of edges.

$$G=(V,E)$$

Ex: airlines for maintaining flight information such as various flight routes, distance between places, etc.

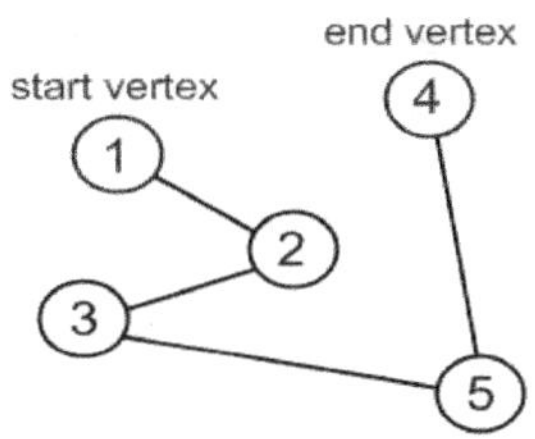

# CHAPTER 2

# ABSTRACT DATA TYPES (ADTS)

Abstract Data Types (ADTs) are user defined data types. It is a mathematical model of the data objects that make up a data type as well as the functions that operate on those data. An ADT has 2 parts:

- A name or type, specifying a set of data (e.g. Dictionary).

- Descriptions of all the operations (or methods) that do things with that type (e.g. find, insert, remove).The descriptions indicate what the operations do, not how they do it.

It can change ADT implementation details without breaking code using ADT. It is a Preferred way of designing and implementing data structures.

It Uses 2 general principles i.e., information hiding and re-usability.

- Information hiding: User data structure should not need to know details of its implementation. We should be able to change implementation without affecting applications that use it. Therefore, implementation information should be hidden.

- Re-usability: If data structure is useful for one application, it is probably useful for another. Therefore, we should design it to be as re-usable as possible.

A data structure is a systematic way of organizing and accessing data from a computer (e.g. array, linked list). Data structures are used to implement ADTs.

## 2.1.  ADT Dictionary

find (key): returns a record with the given key, or null if no record has the given key

insert(key,data): inserts a new record with given key and data ERROR if the dictionary already contains a record with the given key

remove(key): removes the record with the given key ERROR if there is no record with the given key

***Advantages of ADT***

- Easy to debug small routines than large routines.

- Several people to work on modular program simultaneously.

- Well-written modular program places certain dependencies in only one routine, maling changes easier.

*Specification of basic ADTs*

## 2.2.    The List ADT

List of size N: A0, A1, …, AN-1

Each element $A_k$ has a unique position k in the list. Elements can be arbitrarily complex.

### *Operations of List ADT*

1.  PrintList: It is used to print the elements in the list.
2.  MakeEmpty: It makes an list empty.
3.  Find: It returns the position of first occurrence of a key.
4.  Insert and delete: It is used to insert and delete the element.
5.  Find $K^{th}$: It returns element in some position.

    Example: 34,12,52,16,12

    Find (52) = 3

    Insert (X,3) = 34,12,52,X,16,12

    Delete(52) = 34,12,X,16,12

### *The Stack ADT*

Stack = a list where insert and remove take place only at the "top".

Operations involved are Push (insert) element on top of stack, Pop (remove) element from top of stack, Top to return element at top of stack.

### *The Queue ADT*

Queue = a list where insert takes place at the back, but remove takes place at the front.

Operations are Enqueue (insert) element at the back of the queue, Dequeue (remove and return) element from the front of the queue.

### *Linked List*

A linked list is a linear data structure where each element is a separate object. Each element i.e., node of a list is comprising of two items the data field to store values and next filed used to store address of next node and forms a chain.  The last node has a reference to null. The entry point into a linked list is called the head of the list. Linked Lists are used to create trees and graphs. Linked list is a sequence of structure which are not in a contiguous memory location

### *Structure Definition*

struct node

{

int data;

struct node *next;

};

### *Advantages of Linked List*

- They are a dynamic in nature which allocates the memory when required.
- Insertion and deletion operations can be easily implemented.
- Stacks and queues can be easily executed.
- Linked List reduces the access time.

### *Disadvantages of Linked List*

- The memory is wasted as pointers require extra memory for storage.
- No element can be accessed randomly; it has to access each node sequentially.
- Reverse Traversing is difficult in linked list.

### *Applications of Linked List*

- Linked lists are used to implement stacks, queues, graphs, etc.
- Linked lists let you insert elements at the beginning and end of the list.
- In Linked Lists, we don't need to know the size in advance.

## 2.3.  Types of Linked List

1. **Singly Linked List:** Singly linked lists contain nodes which have a data part as well as an address part i.e. next, which points to the next node in sequence of nodes. The operations we can perform on singly linked lists are insertion, deletion and traversal.

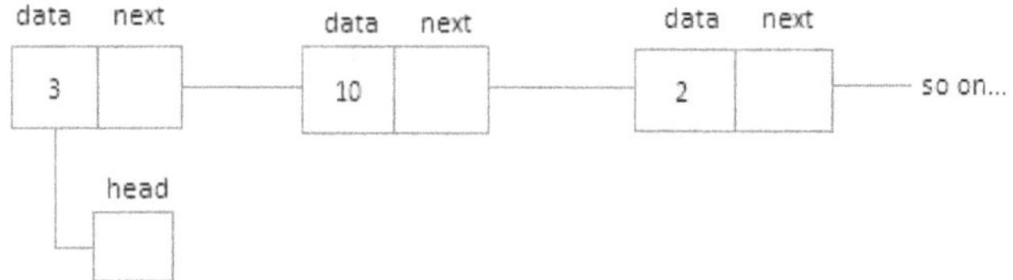

2. **Doubly Linked List:** In a doubly linked list, each node contains two links the first link points to the previous node and the next link points to the next node in the sequence.

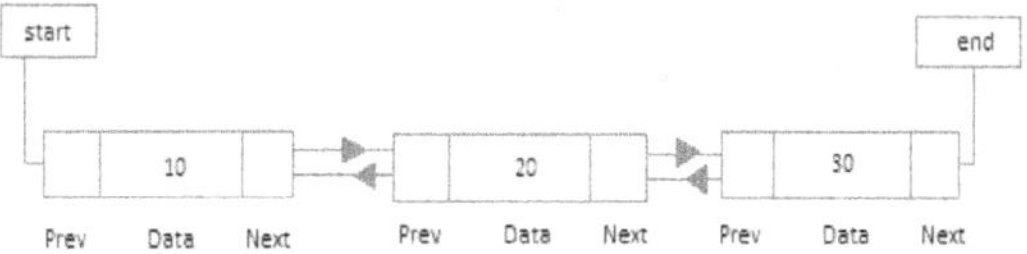

3. **Circular Linked List:** In the circular linked list the last node of the list contains the address of the first node and forms a circular chain.

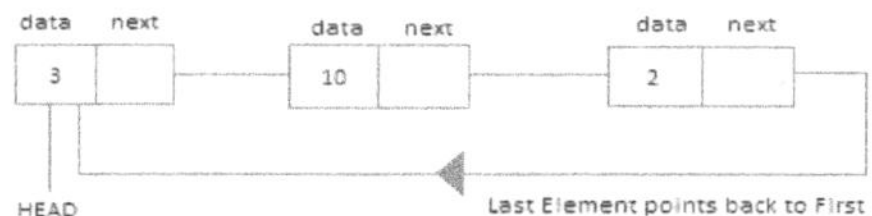

## 2.4. Singly Linked List: [one-way List]

Singly linked lists contain nodes which have a data part as well as an address part i.e. next, which points to the next node in sequence of nodes. The operations we can perform on singly linked lists are insertion, deletion and traversal.

### a. *Routine for Creation of Node*

```
scanf("%d",&e);
head=malloc(sizeof(struct node));
head->data=e;
head->next-NULL;
printf("%d",head);
printf("%d",head->data);
printf("%d",head->next);
tail=head;
{
    printf("enter a value");
    scanf("%d",&d);
    if(d!=0)
    {
        temp=(struct node*)malloc(sizeof(struct node));
```

```
temp->data=d;

temp->next=NULL;

tail->next=temp;
```

100   200
5   200   10
head, tail   temp

```
tail=temp; }
```

## b. *Insert at Front*

```
void insertfront()
{
   printf("\nenter a value:");
   scanf("%d",&d);   temp=malloc (sizeof(struct node));
   temp->data=d;
   temp->next=NULL;
   temp->next=head;
   head=temp;


}
```

5   200   15   300   25
100   200   300
2   100
temp, head

## c. *Insert at Last*

```
void insertlast()
{
   printf("\nenter a value");
   scanf("%d",&d);
   temp=malloc (sizeof(struct node));
   temp->data=d;
   temp->next=NULL;
   tail->next=temp;
   tail=temp;
}
```

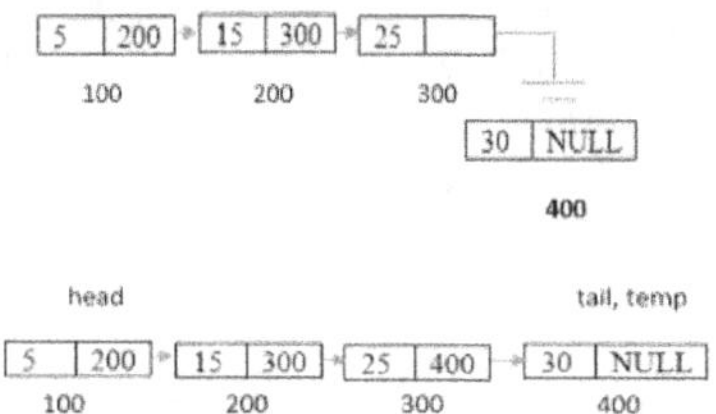

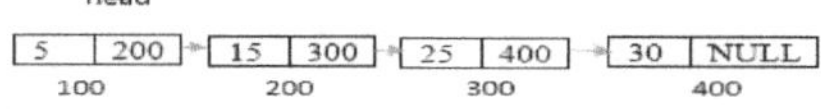

## d. Insert at Middle

```
void insertmiddle()
{
int pos,count=1;
printf("\nenter a value");
scanf("%d",&d);
printf("\n enter the position where data to be inserted");
scanf("%d",&pos);
temp=head;
while(count!=pos)
{
 k1=temp;
temp=temp->next;
count++;
}
 k=malloc(sizeof(struct node));
k->data=d;
k1->next=k;
k->next=temp;
}
```

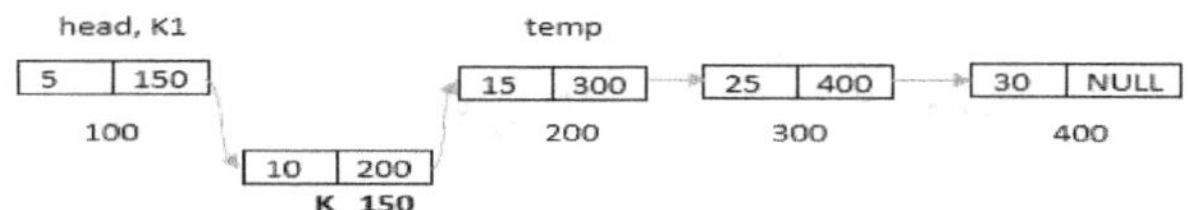

## e. *Delete at Front*

void deletefront()

{

  temp=head;

  head=temp->next;

  free(temp);

}

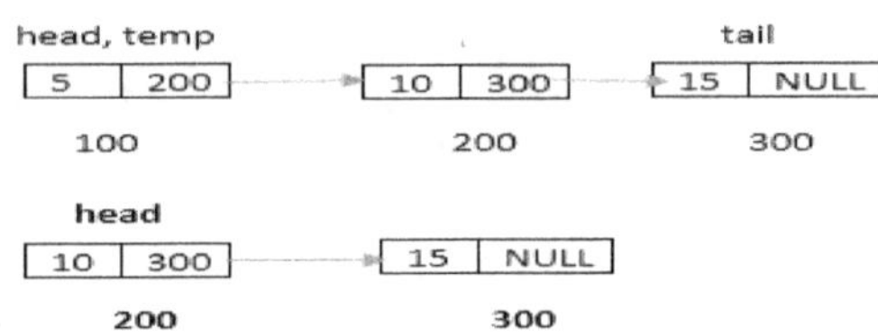



## f. *Delete at Last*

void deletelast()

{

temp=head;

while(temp->next!=null)

{

k1=temp;

temp=temp->next;

}

k1->next=null;

free(temp);

}

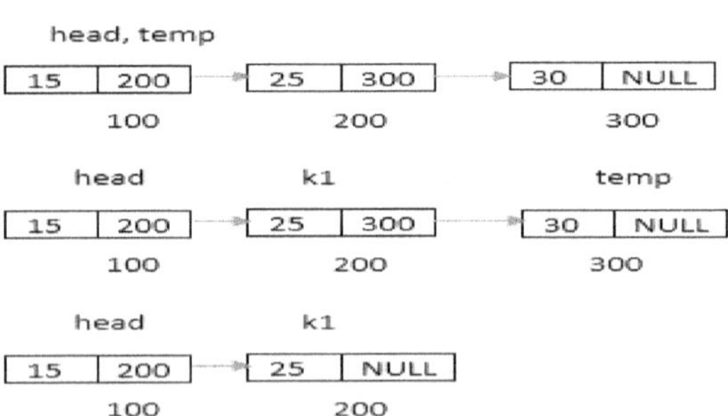

### g. *Delete at Middle*

```c
void deletemiddle()
{
int position,count=1;
printf("enter position");
scanf("%d",&position);
  temp=head;
  while(count!=position)
  {
    k=temp;
    temp=temp->next;
    count++;
}
  k1=temp->next;
  k->next=k1;
  free(temp);
}
```

head, temp, k1

| 5 | 200 | → | 10 | 300 | → | 15 | 400 | → | 20 | NULL |

| 100 | | 200 | | 300 | | 400 |

head

| 5 | 300 | → | 15 | 400 | → | 20 | NULL |

| 100 | | 300 | | 400 |

### h. *Reverse Function*

```c
void reverse()
{
current=head;
prev=NULL;
  while (current != NULL)
  {
    temp  = current->next;
    current->next = prev;
    prev = current;
    current = temp;
  }
  head = prev;
}
```

### i.  *Concatenate Function*

```c
void concaten()
{
  if(head==NULL)
  head=head1;
  else
  {
    if(head1!=NULL)
    tail->next=head1;
  }
}
```

### 2.4.1.  *Program for Linear Linked List*

```c
#include<stdio.h>
#include<conio.h>
void createnode();
void display();
struct node
{
   int data;
   struct node *next;
};
typedef struct node *list;
list head, tail,temp,k,k1;
int s,d,t,a,m,position,count=0;
void createnode();
void display();
void deletemiddle();
void deletefront();
void insertfront();
void insertlast();
void reverse();
void createnode()
{
   printf("enter a value");
```

```c
scanf("%d",&d);
head=(struct node*)malloc(sizeof(struct node));
head->data=d;
head->next=NULL;
tail=head;
do
{
  printf("enter  a value");
  scanf("%d",&t);
  if(t!=0)
  {
    temp=(struct node*)malloc(sizeof(struct node));
    temp->data=t;
    temp->next=NULL;
    tail->next=temp;
    tail=temp;
  }
}while(t!=0);
}
void createnode1()
{
  printf("enter a value");
  scanf("%d",&e);
  head1= (struct node *)malloc(sizeof(struct node));
  head1->data=d;
  head1->next=NULL;
  tail1=head1;
  do
  {
    printf("enter  a value");
    scanf("%d",&f);
    if(f!=0)
    {
      temp1=(struct node*)malloc(sizeof(struct node));
```

```c
            temp1->data=f;
            temp1->next=NULL;
            tail1->next=temp1;
            tail1=temp1;
        }
    }while(f!=0);
}
void display()
{
    temp=head;
    while(temp!=NULL)
    {
        printf("%d",temp->data);
        temp=temp->next;
    }
}
void insertfront()
{
    printf("\nenter a value:");
    scanf("%d",&a);
    temp=(struct node*)malloc(sizeof(struct node));
    temp->data=a;
    temp->next=head;
    head=temp;
}
void insertlast()
{
    printf("\nenter a value");
    scanf("%d",&s);
    temp=(struct node*)malloc(sizeof(struct node));
    temp->data=s;
    temp->next=NULL;
    tail->next=temp;
    tail=temp;
```

```c
}
void insertmiddle()
{
 printf("\nenter a value");
 scanf("%d",&m);
 printf("\nenter position");
 scanf("%d",&pos);
 temp=head;
 while(count!=pos)
{
 k1=temp;
 temp=temp->next;
 count++;
}
 k=malloc(sizeof(struct node));
k->data=m;
k1->next=k;
k->next=temp;
}
void deletefront()
{
  temp=head;
  head=temp->next;
  free(temp);
}
void deletemiddle()
{
  printf("enter position");
  scanf("%d",position);
  temp=head;
  while(count!=position)
  {
    k=temp;
    temp=temp->next;
```

```c
        count++;
      k1=temp->next;
    }
    free(temp);
    k->next=k1;
}
void reverse()
{
current=head;
prev=NULL;
    while (current != NULL)
    {
      temp  = current->next;
      current->next = prev;
      prev = current;
      current = temp;
    }
    head = prev;
}
void concaten()
{

  if(head==NULL)
    head=head1;
  else
  {
    if(head1!=NULL)
    tail->next=head1;
      }
  }
void main()
{
  int n;
  while(n!=9)
```

```c
{
printf("enter choice");
scanf("%d",&n);
switch (n)
{
   case 1:createnode();
   break;
   case 2:display();
   break;
   case 3:insertfront();
   display();
   break;
   case 4:insertlast();
   display();
   break;
   case 5:deletefront();
   display();
   break;
   case 6:deletemiddle();
   display();
   break;
   case 7:reverse();
   display();
   break;
   case 8: createnode1();
   display();
   concaten();
   display();
   break;
   default:printf("invalid");
   break;
  }
 }
}
```

## 2.5.    Doubly Linked Lists

A doubly linked list is a list that contains links to next and previous nodes. Unlike singly linked lists where traversal is only one way, doubly linked lists allow traversals in both ways. A generic doubly linked list node can be designed as

```
typedef struct node {
int data;
struct node* next;
struct node* prev;
} node;
```

- Doubly Linked List contains a link element called first and last.
- Each link carries a data field(s) and a link field called next.
- Each link is linked with its next link using its next link.
- Each link is linked with its previous link using its previous link.
- The last link carries a link as null to mark the end of the list.

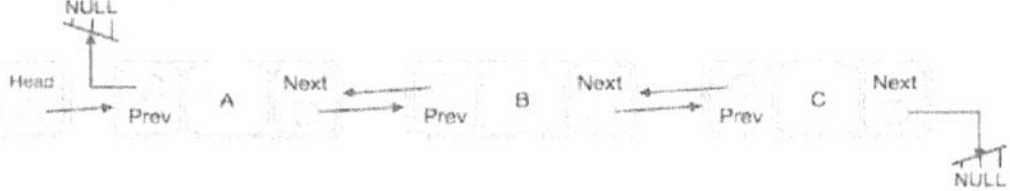


### *Insertion at the Front Operation*

```
void insertFirst(int key, int data)
{
struct node *link = malloc(sizeof(struct node)); //create a link
  link->key = key;
  link->data = data;
  if(isEmpty())
{
    last = link;   //make it the last link
  } else {
    //update first prev link
    head->prev = link;
  }
    link->next = head; //point it to old first link
    head = link; //point first to new first link
  }
```

### Deletion Operation

```
struct node* deleteFirst()
{
struct node *tempLink = head; //save reference to first link
if(head->next== NULL){
last= NULL;
}else
{
   head->next->prev = NULL;
}
  head = head->next;
return tempLink;//return the deleted link
}
```

### Insertion at the End

```
void insertLast(int key,int data)
{
struct node *link =(struct node*) malloc(sizeof(struct node));
  link->key = key;
  link->data = data;
if(isEmpty()){
last= link; //make it the last link
}else{
last->next= link;//make link a new last link
    link->prev =last; //mark old last node as prev of new link
}
last= link;//point last to new last node
}
```

## 2.6.    Circular Linked List

Circular Linked List is a variation of Linked list in which the first element points to the last element and the last element points to the first element.

Both Singly Linked List and Doubly Linked List can be made into a circular linked list.

### Singly Linked List as Circular

In singly linked list, the next pointer of the last node points to the first node.

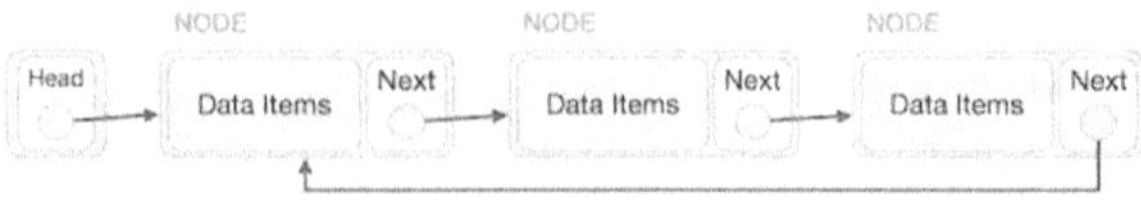

### Doubly Linked List as Circular

In doubly linked list, the next pointer of the last node points to the first node and the previous pointer of the first node points to the last node making the circular in both directions.

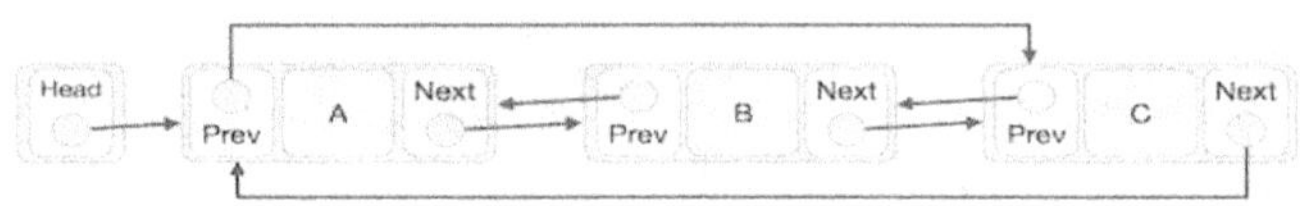

- The last link's next points to the first link of the list in both cases of singly as well as doubly linked list.
- The first link's previous points to the last of the list in case of doubly linked list.

Basic Operations:

Following are the important operations supported by a circular list.

- insert – Inserts an element at the start of the list.
- delete – Deletes an element from the start of the list.
- display – Displays the list.

### Insertion Operation

```
void insertFirst(int key,int data){
struct node *link =(struct node*) malloc(sizeof(struct node));
  link->key = key;
  link->data= data;
if(isEmpty()){
    head = link;
    head->next= head;
}else{
  link->next= head; //point it to old first node
  head = link;//point first to new first node
}
}
```

### Deletion Operation

```
struct node * deleteFirst(){
struct node *tempLink = head;
if(head->next== head){
   head = NULL;
return tempLink;
}
   head = head->next; //mark next to first link as first
   return tempLink; //return the deleted link
}
```

### Display Operation

```
void printList(){
struct node *ptr = head;
  printf("\n[ ");
//start from the beginning
if(head != NULL){
while(ptr->next!= ptr){
    printf("(%d,%d) ",ptr->key,ptr->data);
    ptr = ptr->next;
}
}
  printf(" ]");
}
```

## 2.7.    Application of Linked List

- Linked Lists can be used to implement Stacks, Queues.
- Linked Lists can also be used to implement Graphs. (Adjacency list representation of Graph).
- Implementing Hash Tables: Each Bucket of the hash table can itself be a linked list. (Open chain hashing).
- Undo functionality in Photoshop or Word. Linked list of states.
- A polynomial can be represented in an array or in a linked list by simply storing the coefficient and exponent of each term.

- However, for any polynomial operation, such as addition or multiplication of polynomials, linked list representation is easier to deal with.
- Linked lists are useful for dynamic memory allocation.
- The real-life application where the circular linked list is used is our Personal Computers, where multiple applications are running.
- All the running applications are kept in a circular linked list and the OS gives a fixed time slot to all for running. The Operating System keeps on iterating over the linked list until all the applications are completed.

## *Polynomial ADT*

A Polynomial, $P(x)$ is an expression, the variable x of the form $ax^n+bx^{n-1}+cx^{n-2}+\ldots\ldots gx+h$) where $a,b,c,\ldots\ldots g$, h are real numbers and n is a non-negative number(degree of the polynomial).

In polynomial expression, there are 2 parts. one is coefficient and the other is exponent.

Example:

$50x^5+40x^4-30x^3+20x^2-10x$

Here (50,40, -30,20, -10) are co-efficient and (5,4,3,2,1) are exponents.

The **structure of polynomial** can be defined using linked list as

struct poly
{
int coeff;
int pow;
struct poly *next;
} *list 1, *list 2;

## *Program for Polynomial Addition*

```
#include<stdio.h>
#include<malloc.h>
#include<conio.h>
struct link{
int coeff;
int pow;
struct link *next;
};
```

```c
struct link *poly1=NULL,*poly2=NULL,*poly=NULL;
void create(struct link *node)
{
char ch;
do
{
 printf("\n enter coeff:");
 scanf("%d",&node->coeff);
 printf("\n enter power:");
 scanf("%d",&node->pow);
 node->next=(struct link*)malloc(sizeof(struct link));
 node=node->next;
 node->next=NULL;
 printf("\n continue(y/n):");
 ch=getch();
}
while(ch=='y'|| ch=='Y');
}
void show(struct link *node)
{
while(node->next!=NULL)
{
 printf("%dx^%d",node->coeff,node->pow);
 node=node->next;
if(node->next!=NULL)
  printf("+");
}
}
void polyadd(struct link *poly1,struct link *poly2,struct link *poly)
{
while(poly1->next&& poly2->next)
{
if(poly1->pow>poly2->pow)
{
```

```c
        poly->pow=poly1->pow;
        poly->coeff=poly1->coeff;
        poly1=poly1->next;
    }
    elseif(poly1->pow<poly2->pow)
    {
        poly->pow=poly2->pow;
        poly->coeff=poly2->coeff;
        poly2=poly2->next;
    }
    else
    {
        poly->pow=poly1->pow;
        poly->coeff=poly1->coeff+poly2->coeff;
        poly1=poly1->next;
        poly2=poly2->next;
    }
        poly->next=(struct link *)malloc(sizeof(struct link));
        poly=poly->next;
        poly->next=NULL;
    }
    while(poly1->next|| poly2->next)
    {
    if(poly1->next)
    {
        poly->pow=poly1->pow;
        poly->coeff=poly1->coeff;
        poly1=poly1->next;
    }
    if(poly2->next)
    {
        poly->pow=poly2->pow;
        poly->coeff=poly2->coeff;
        poly2=poly2->next;
```

```c
}
    poly->next=(struct link *)malloc(sizeof(struct link));
    poly=poly->next;
    poly->next=NULL;
}
}
main()
{
char ch;
do{
    poly1=(struct link *)malloc(sizeof(struct link));
    poly2=(struct link *)malloc(sizeof(struct link));
    poly=(struct link *)malloc(sizeof(struct link));
    printf("\nenter 1st number:");
    create(poly1);
    printf("\nenter 2nd number:");
    create(poly2);
    printf("\n1st Number:");
    show(poly1);
    printf("\n2nd Number:");
    show(poly2);
    polyadd(poly1,poly2,poly);
    printf("\nAdded polynomial:");
    show(poly);
    printf("\n add two more numbers:");
    ch=getch();
}
while(ch=='y'|| ch=='Y');
}
```

### Multilists

Doubly-linked lists are a special of multi-linked lists:

- each node has just 2 pointers
- they are exact inverses of each other

Multi-linked list: each node can have any number of pointers to other nodes. Each pointer may or may not have an inverse.

Example:

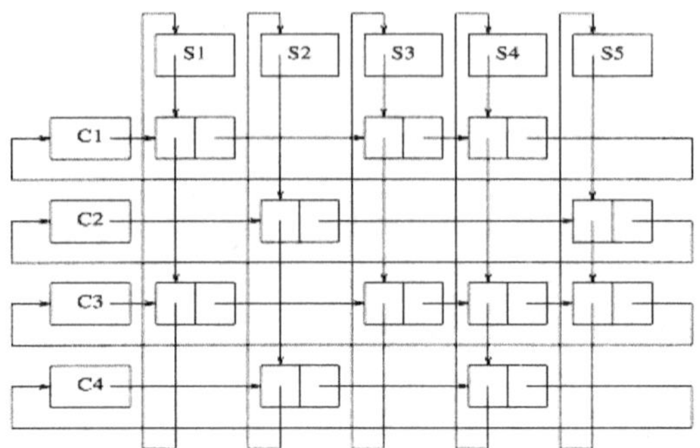

It is useful to maintain student registration.

Two reports can be generated in this student registration system. They are

- List of registration for each class.
- The Classes that each student is registered for.

For example, if we want to create a report on list of students registered for classes, it can be determined using the link.

The student registered for class C1 are S1, S3, S4.

The student registered for class C3 are S1, S3, S4, S5

Similarly, the report can be based on individual student registration.

The student S1 registers on classes C1, C3

The student S4 registers on classes C1, C2, C3

███████████████████████ **CHAPTER 3** ███████████████████████

# STACK AND QUEUE ADT

## 3.1. Stack Model

A stack is a linear data structure which is used to store data in a particular order, where insertion and deletion of items takes place at only one end called top of the stack. It is an ordered list of similar data types.

It is an abstract data type that serves as a collection of elements. It is very useful data structure in C Programming. It follows Last In First Out (LIFO) order or First In Last Out (FILO) order.

### *The Operations that can be Performed on a Stack are*

- Push operation which inserts an element into the stack.
- Pop operation which removes the last element that was added into the stack.
- Peep or Peek operation which returns the value of the top the stack.

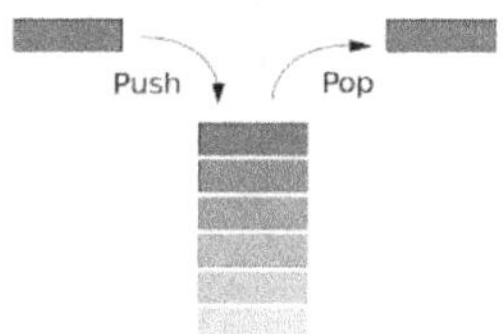


A stack in C may declared as structure containing two objects.

- An array to hold the elements of the stack.
- A variable top to hold the topmost element of the stack.

### *Disadvantages of Stack*

- Memory Space is wasted if we store less number of items in the array than maximum size.
- Limitations in storing the items into the stack.

## 3.2. Implementation of Stack Using Array

Array cannot be a stack; it can be home of a stack. Stack is a dynamic objects whose size is constantly changing as items are pushed and popped. A stack data structure can be implemented using one dimensional array.

This implementation is very simple, just define a one-dimensional array of specific size and insert or delete the values into that array by using Last In First Out(LIFO) principle with the help of a variable 'top'. Initially top is set to -1.

## *Example*

Consider Stack with following details

| *Field* | *Value* |
|---|---|
| Size of the Stack | 6 |
| Maximum Value of Stack Top | 5 |
| Minimum Value of Stack Top | 0 |
| Value of Top when Stack is Empty | -1 |
| Value of Top when Stack is Full | 5 |

## *Step 1: Empty Stack (Initial Condition)*

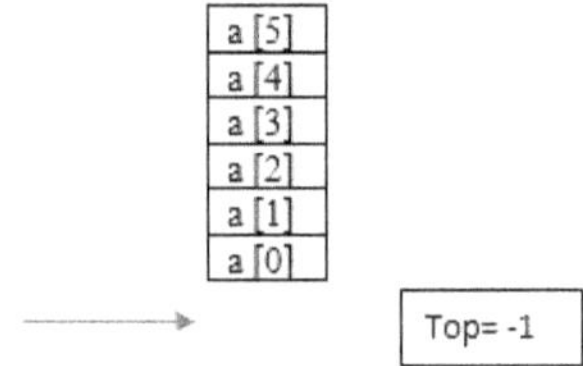


When stack is empty, top=-1

## *Step 2: Push Operation*

The process of inserting a new element onto the top of the stack.

If first element 5 is inserted, then topmost position will be incremented by 1. Then top pointer will move from a [-1] to the position a[0].

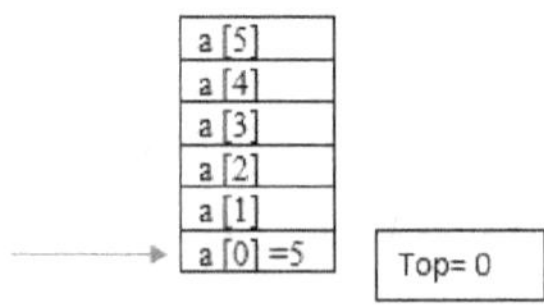


If Second element 10 is inserted, then top pointer will move to the position a[1] from a[0].

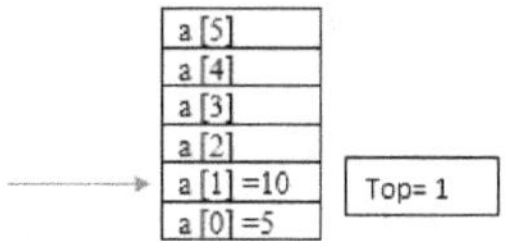

## Step 3: Pop Operation

The process of deleting an element from the top of the stack.

If element 10 in a[1] is deleted, then topmost position will be decremented by 1. Then top pointer will move to the position a[0] from a[1].

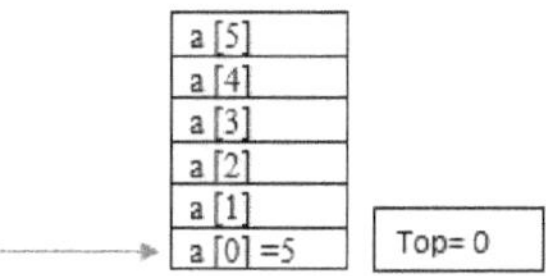

## Step 4: Peep Operation

It returns the topmost Element of the Stack.

TOP ELEMNET = PEEP OR PEEK

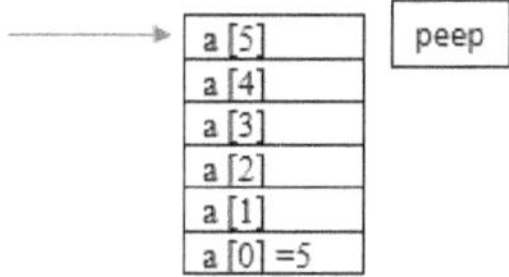

Procedure (Stack Implementation Using Arrays):

- Declare an array S of size N.
- Declare the variable top, i, item, stack[N]
- Initialize top= -1 (if top = -1 means stack is empty)
- Declare the function push, pop, display and exit
- To push an item (entry) onto the stack, check whether the stack is full or not
- *Stack Full operation(Stack Overflow)*
    - If top>=N means stack is full
- *Push operation:* The function push will increment top value by one after adding every element into the stack
    - Inserts new item at the top of the stack

- top = top +1
  - stack(top)=item
- *Pop operation:* The function pop will decrement top value by one after deleting every element from the Stack deletes the values from the stack. Popping an entry from the stack into ITEM requires
  - item =Stack(top)
  - top = top -1
- *Stack Empty operation (Stack Underflow)*
  - For empty stack the condition will be top ==-1

### *Program for Stack Implementation Using Arrays*

```c
#include<stdio.h>
#define size 5
void push();
void pop();
void display();
void peek();
int st[size],top=-1,d,temp;
void push()
{
  if(top>=size)
  {
    printf("stack is full");
  }
    else
  {
      printf("\n enter elements");
      scanf("%d",&d);
      top++;
      st[top]=d;
  }
}
void pop()
{
  if(top==-1)
```

```c
{
    printf("stack is empty");
}
    else
    {
    temp=st[top];
    top=top-1;
    printf("\nno deleted is %d",temp);
    }
}
void peek()
{
    temp=st[top];
    printf("%d",temp);
}
void display()
{int i;
    for(i=top;i>=0;i--)
    {
        printf("%d",st[i]) ;
    }
}
int main()
{
    int ch;
    while(1)
    {
    printf("\n1.push \n2.pop\n3.peek");
    printf("\nenter your choice");
    scanf("%d",&ch);
    switch(ch)
    {
        case 1:push();
        break;
```

```
            case 2:
                pop();
                break;
            case 3:
                peek();
                break;
            case 4:
                display();
                break;
            case 5:
                exit(0);
                break;
        }
    }
    getch();
}
```

## 3.3.    Implementation of Stack Using Linked List

- A data member to store the pointer to the top of the stack
- The next element of the last node should contain the value NULL

### *Structure Definition*

```
Struct node
{
int data;
struct data * next;
}*top=NULL,*temp;
```

### *Push Operation*

Insert an element into the stack.

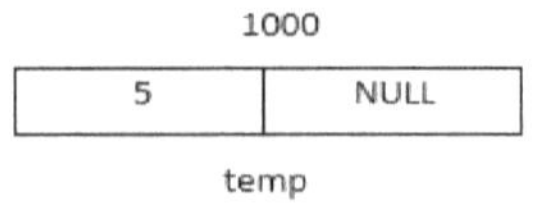

```
scanf("%d", &e);          //To get an value to insert into an array
temp = malloc(sizeof(struct node));   //Allocate memory for head(i.e.,temp=1000)
temp-> data=e;            //Insert the value 5 into data field(i.e.,temp->data=5)
temp-> next=top;          //The value of top is fixed into temp->next(i.e.,top=NULL)
top=temp;                 //The value of temp is moved to top(i.e.,top=1000)
```

| 15 | 2000 | | 10 | 1000 | | 5 | NULL |
|----|------|--|----|------|--|---|------|
| 3000 | | | 2000 | | | 1000 | |

## Pop Operation

```
if(top==NULL)
    printf("stack is empty");
  else
  {
    temp=top;
    printf("%d ",temp->data);
    top=temp->next;
    free(temp);
  }
```

## Tracing

```
1) temp=3000      2) temp=2000      3) temp=1000      4) if(top==NULL)
   temp->data=15     temp->data=10     temp->data=5   {
   top=2000          top=1000          top=NULL        Stack is empty
   free(3000)        free(2000)        free(1000)      }
```

## Program for Stack Using Linked List

```c
#include<stdio.h>
struct node
{
  int data;
  struct node *next;
}*top=NULL,*temp;
void push()
{
  int e;
```

```c
    printf("\nenter element");
    scanf("%d",&e);
    temp=malloc(sizeof(struct node));
    temp->data=e;
    temp->next=top;
    top=temp;
}
void pop()
{
  if(top==NULL)

    printf("stack is empty");
  else
  {
    printf("\nelement popped %d",temp->data);
    temp=temp->next;
    free(top);
    top=temp;
  }
}
void display()
{
  if(top==NULL)
  {
    printf("\nstack is empty");
  }
  else
  {
    while(temp!=NULL)
    {
    top=temp;
    printf("%d",temp->data);
    temp=temp->next;
    }
```

```c
}
}
int main()
{
  int ch;
  while(1)
  {
    printf("\n1.push\n2.pop\n3.display\n4.exit");
    printf("\nenter your choice");
    scanf("%d",&ch);
    switch(ch)
    {
      case 1:push();
      break;
      case 2:pop();
      break;
      case 3:display();
      break;
      case 4:exit(0);
      break;
    }
  }
```

### *Analysis of Stack*

The time complexities for various operations that can be performed on the Stack data structure.

- Push Operation : O(1)
- Pop Operation : O(1)
- Top Operation : O(1)
- Search Operation : O(n)

## 3.4.    Application of Stack

1. Expression Evolution
2. Expression conversion
3. Balancing Parenthesis

## 1. Expression Evolution

An expression is a collection of operators and operands that represents a specific value.

In above definition, operator is a symbol which performs a particular task like arithmetic operation or logical operation or conditional operation etc.

Operands are the values on which the operators can perform the task. Here operand can be a direct value or variable or address of memory location.

### Expression Types

Based on the operator position, expressions are divided into 3 types. They are as follows

a.   Infix Expression

b.   Postfix Expression

c.   Prefix Expression

### a.  Infix Expression

In infix expression, operator is used in between operands. The general structure of an Infix expression is as follows

Operand1 Operator Operand2

Example: (a+b)

### b.  Postfix Expression

In postfix expression, operator is used after operands. We can say that *"Operator follows the Operands"*. The general structure of Postfix expression is as follows

Operand1 Operand2 Operator

Example: ab+

### c.  Prefix Expression

In prefix expression, operator is used before operands. We can say that *"Operands follows the Operator"*.

The general structure of Prefix expression is as follows

Operator Operand1 Operand2

Example: +ab

## 2. *Expression Conversion*

Any expression can be represented using three types of expressions (Infix, Postfix and Prefix). We can also convert one type of expression to another type of expression like Infix to Postfix, Infix to Prefix, Postfix to Prefix and vice versa.

To convert any Infix expression into Postfix or Prefix expression we can use the following procedure.

- Find all the operators in the given Infix Expression.
- Find the order of operators evaluated according to their Operator precedence.
- Convert each operator into required type of expression (Postfix or Prefix) in the same order.

### *Example*

Consider the following Infix Expression to be converted into Postfix Expression.

$$A=B+C*D$$

Step 1: The Operators in the given Infix Expression : = , + , *

Step 2: The Order of Operators according to their preference : * , + , =

Step 3: Now, convert the first operator * ----- A = B + CD *

Step 4: Convert the next operator + ----- A= BCD* +

Step 5: Convert the next operator = ----- A BCD*+ =

Finally, given Infix Expression is converted into Postfix Expression as follows...

$$A\ BCD*+\ =$$

### *Infix to Postfix Conversion Using Stack Data Structures*

To convert Infix Expression into Postfix Expression using a stack data structure, we can use the following steps.

Step 1: Read all the symbols one by one from left to right in the given Infix Expression.

Step 2: If the reading symbol is operand, then directly print it to the result (Output).

Step 3: If the reading symbol is left parenthesis '(', then Push it on to the Stack.

Step 4: If the reading symbol is right parenthesis ')', then Pop all the contents of stack until respective left parenthesis is poped and print each poped symbol to the result.

Step 5: If the reading symbol is operator (+ , - , * , / etc.,), then Push it on to the Stack. However, first pop the operators which are already on the stack that have higher or equal precedence than current operator and print them to the result.

### *Example*

Consider the following Infix Expression.

$$(A+B)*(C+D)$$

The given infix expression can be converted into postfix expression using Stack Data Structure as follows

| Reading Character | Stack | Postfix expression |
| --- | --- | --- |
| Initially | Stack is Empty | Empty |
| ( | Push '(' <br> top → ( | Empty |
| A | No operation so 'A' is operand <br> top → ( | A |
| + | + has lower priority than '('so, push '+' <br> top → + <br> ( | A |

| Input | Operation | Stack (top →) | Output |
|---|---|---|---|
| B | No operation so 'B' is operand | +, ( | AB |
| ) | Pop all elements till we Reach '(' Pop '+' Pop '(' | (empty) | AB+ |
| * | Stack is empty and '*' is operator so push '*' into the stack | * | AB+ |
| ( | push '(' | (, * | AB+ |
| C | No operation so 'C' is operand | (, * | AB+C |
| - | '- 'has lower priority than '('so push '- ' | -, (, * | AB+C |

| | | |
|---|---|---|
| D | **No operation so 'D' is operand** → top<br><br>( - / ( / * stack ) | AB+CD |
| ) | **Pop all elements till we reach '('**<br>**Pop '+'**<br>**Push '('**<br><br>top → ( * stack ) | AB+CD- |
| $ | Pop all elements till stack becomes empty | AB+CD-* |

### *Postfix Expression Evaluation*

A postfix expression is a collection of operators and operands in which the operator is placed after the operands. That means, in a postfix expression the operator follows the operands.

Postfix Expression has following general structure

Operand1 Operand2Operator

Postfix expression can be evaluated using the Stack data structure. To evaluate a postfix expression using Stack data structure we can use the following steps.

Step 1: Read all the symbols one by one from left to right in the given Postfix Expression

Step 2: If the reading symbol is operand, then push it on to the Stack.

Step 3: If the reading symbol is operator (+,-, * , / etc.,), then perform two pop operations and store the two popped operands in two different variables (operand1 and operand2). Then perform reading symbol operation using operand1 and operand2 and push result back on to the Stack.

Step 4: Finally perform a pop operation and display the popped value as final result.

## *Example*

Consider the following Expression.

Infix Expression: (5+3) * (8-2)

Postfix Expression:  53+82-*

| Reading Character | Stack | Evaluated expression |
|---|---|---|
| Initially | Stack is Empty | Empty |
| 5 | Push (5)<br>5 | Empty |
| 3 | Push (3)<br>3<br>5 | Empty |
| + | Value 1= pop()<br>Value 2 =pop()<br>result= value 2 + value 1<br>Push (result<br>8 | Value 1=pop() //3<br>Value 2=pop()//5<br>Result=5+3; //8<br>Push(8)<br><br>(5+3) |

| | | | |
|---|---|---|---|
| 8 | Push (8) | | (5+3) |
| 2 | Push (2) | | (5+3) |
| - | Value 1= pop()<br>Value 2 =pop()<br>result= value 2 - value 1<br>Push (result) | 6<br>8 | Value 1=pop()<br>//2<br>Value 2=pop()//8<br>Result=8-2; //6<br>Push(6)<br>(8-2)<br>(5+3),(8-2) |
| * | Value 1= pop()<br>Value 2 =pop()<br>result= value 2 * value 1<br>Push (result) | 48 | Value 1=pop()<br>//6<br>Value 2=pop()//8<br>Result=8*6; //48<br>Push(48)<br>(6*8)<br>(5+3)*(8-2) |
| $<br>End of Expression | result=pop() | | 48 |

Postfix Expression 53+82-* value is 48

### *Examples*

1.  a+b*c+(d*e+f)*g = abc*+de*f+g*+
2.  (a+b)*c = ab+c*
3.  a+b*c = abc*+
4.  (a+b)/(c-d) = ab+cd-/
5.  a*b+c/d = ab*cd/+

### *Program for Expression Evaluation*

```
#define SIZE 50  /* Size of Stack */
#include <ctype.h>
ints[SIZE];
inttop=-1;     /* Global declarations */
push(intelem)
{               /* Function for PUSH operation */
 s[++top]=elem;
}
intpop()
{               /* Function for POP operation */
 return(s[top--]);
}
main()
{                /* Main Program */
charpofx[50],ch;
inti=0,op1,op2;
printf("\n\nRead the Postfix Expression ? ");
scanf("%s",pofx);
while( (ch=pofx[i++]) != '\0')
{
if(isdigit(ch)) push(ch-'0'); /* Push the operand */
else
{     /* Operator,pop two  operands */
 op2=pop();
 op1=pop();
 switch(ch)
 {
```

```
case'+':push(op1+op2);break;
case'-':push(op1-op2);break;
case'*':push(op1*op2);break;
case'/':push(op1/op2);break;
    }
   }
  }
printf("\n Given Postfix Expn: %s\n",pofx);
printf("\n Result after Evaluation: %d\n",s[top]);
 }
```

### 3. Balancing Parenthesis

Balancing parenthesis is one of the notation for an mathematical expression. The advantage of using Balancing parenthesis is to check whether the given expression is balanced or not.

As you process symbols from left to right, the most recent opening parenthesis must match the next closing symbol. Also, the first opening symbol processed may have to wait until the very last symbol for its match. Closing symbols match opening symbols in the reverse order of their appearance, they match from the inside out.

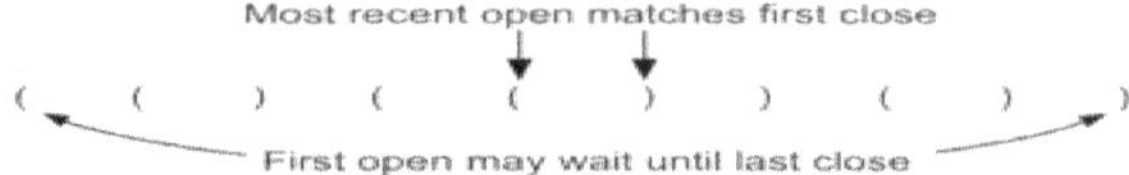


Given a string of characters '(' and ')', we need to find if they form a valid parenthesis, that is to say, find out if there are matching pairs or not. This known as parenthesis matching problem. This problem is also known as *Onion Peeling Problem*

### Examples

1. ()() : valid
2. (() : Invalid, not matching parenthesis
3. ((())) : Valid

### Procedure

- Make an empty stack
- Read the characters until end of file
- If the character is an opening parenthesis (symbol), push it onto the stack

- If it is a closing parenthesis (symbol),

  - Then if the stack is empty report an error

  - Else, pop the stack.

- If the parenthesis (symbol), is not the corresponding opening symbol

  - Then report an error

- At the end of file, if the stack is not empty report an error

- If the parenthesis (symbol), is corresponds to the opening symbol

  - Then display the given expression is balanced

### *Program for Evaluating Balancing Parenthesis*

```c
#include <stdio.h>
#include<conio.h>
#define MAX 20
#define true 1
#define false 0
int top = -1; /*top pointer for stack*/
int stack[MAX];
void push(char);/*function prototypes*/
char pop();
int main()
{
char exp[MAX],temp;
int i,valid=true;
printf("Enter an algebraic expression : ");
gets(exp);
for(i=0;i<=MAX;i++)
{
if(exp[i]=='(' || exp[i]=='{' || exp[i]=='[')
push( exp[i] );
if(exp[i]==')' || exp[i]=='}' || exp[i]==']')
if(top == -1)
valid=false;
else
{
temp=pop();
```

```c
if( exp[i]==')' && (temp=='{' || temp=='[') )
valid=false;
if( exp[i]=='}' && (temp=='(' || temp=='[') )
valid=false;
if( exp[i]==']' && (temp=='(' || temp=='{') )
valid=false;
}
}
if(top >= 0)
valid=false;
if( valid==true )
printf("Valid expression...\n");
else
printf("Invalid expression...\n");
return 0;
}
void push(char item)
{
if(top == (MAX-1))
printf("Stack Overflow\n");
else
{
top=top+1;
stack[top] = item;
}
}
char pop()
{
if(top == -1)
printf("Stack Underflow\n");
else
return(stack[top--]);
return 0;
}
```

## 3.5.  Queue Model

Queue is also an abstract data type or a linear data structure, in which the first element is inserted at one end called REAR (also called tail), and the deletion takes place at other end called as FRONT(also called head).Queue follows First-In-First-Out methodology, i.e., the data item stored first will be accessed first.

A real-world example of queue can be a single-lane one-way road, where the vehicle enters first, exits first. More real-world examples can be seen as queues at the ticket windows and bus-stops.

### *Operations in Queue*

1.  Enqueue to insert an item into the queue
2.  Dequeue is used to remove an item from the queue.
3.  Queue Overflow-If maximum size of the array exist Queue Overflow occurs.
4.  Queue Underflow-If no element in the array i.e., if queue empty, then Queue Underflow occurs.

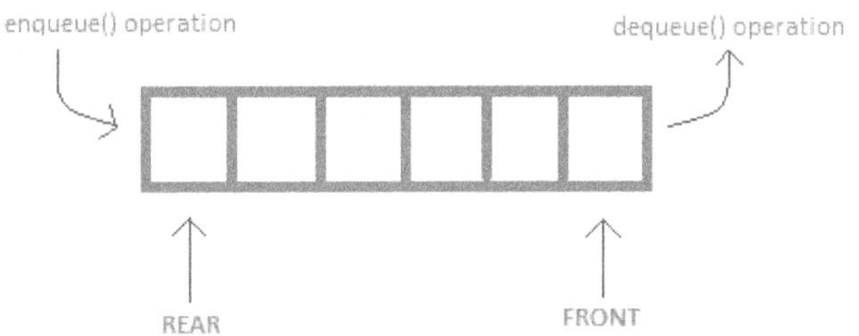


enqueue( ) is the operation for adding an element into Queue.

dequeue( ) is the operation for removing an element from Queue .

**QUEUE DATA STRUCTURE**

### *Basic Features of Queue*

- Like Stack, Queue is also an ordered list of elements of similar data types.
- Queue is a FIFO (First in First Out) structure.
- Once a new element is inserted into the Queue, all the elements inserted before the new element in the queue must be removed, to remove the new element.
- Peek ( ) function is often used to return the value of first element without dequeuing it.

### *Applications of Queue*

- Serving requests on a single shared resource, like a printer, CPU task scheduling etc.
- In real life, Call Centre phone systems will use Queues, to hold people calling them in an order, until a service representative is free.
- Handling of interrupts in real-time systems. The interrupts are handled in the same order as they arrive, first come first served.

### *Types of Queue*

1. Simple or Linear Queue.
2. Circular Queue
3. Deque
4. Priority Queue.

### *Implementation Ways of Queue*

Queue data structure can be implemented in two ways. They are as follows.

1. Using Array
2. Using Linked List

When a queue is implemented using array, that queue can organize only limited number of elements. When a queue is implemented using linked list, that queue can organize unlimited number of elements.

## 3.6.   Implementation of Queue Using Array: [Linear Queue]

Initially the head(FRONT) and the tail(REAR) of the queue points to -1 i.e., Front==-1, Rear==-1.

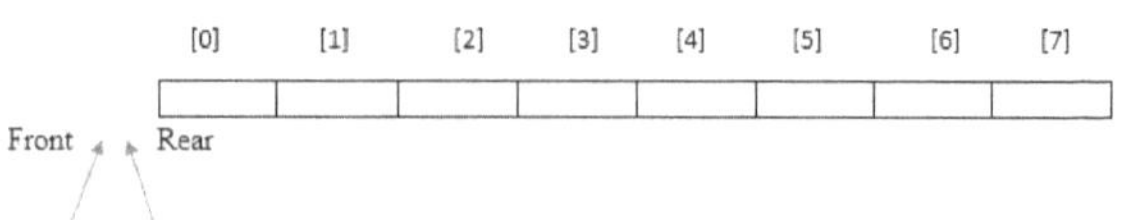

As we add elements to the queue, the Rear keeps on moving ahead, always pointing to the position where the next element will be inserted, while the Front remains at the first index[0].

i.e., Front=0, Rear=Rear+1;

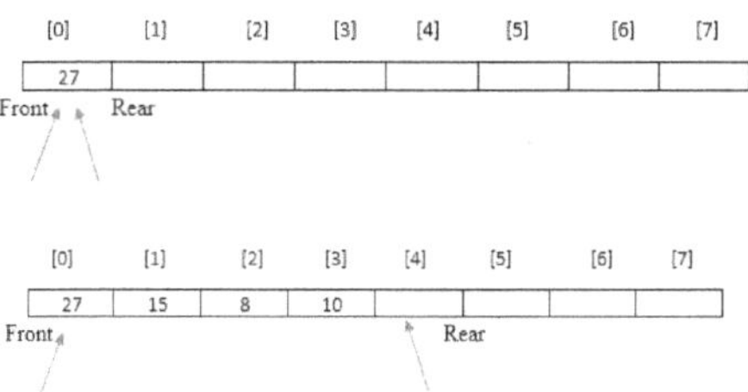

While removing an element from the queue, the Front pointer moves to the next position.

i.e., Front=Front+1;

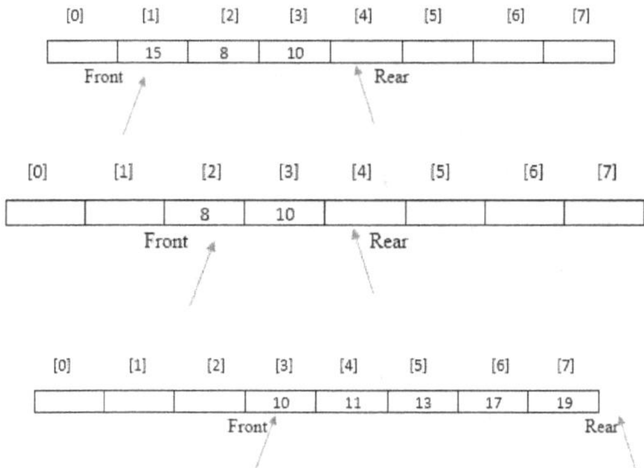

In the case of deletion from the front end, the data's are deleted but the space of the queue is not utilized for the further storage.

Even if the queue has empty cells then also we cannot insert any new element because the insertion has to be done from one side only(i.e. rear or tail) and deletion has to be done from another side (i.e., front or head).This is the main drawback in case of Linear Queue.

The major problem with the queue implemented using array is, it will work for only fixed number of data. That means, the amount of data must be specified in the beginning itself.

Queue using array is not suitable when we don't know the size of data which we are going to use. So, this problem is solved in case of a circular queue. Even if the rear is full but there is space at the front end, then the data can be stored in the front end until the queue overflows.

### Procedure (Queue Implementation Using Arrays)

- Declare an array Q of size N.
- Declare the function insert, delete, and display
    - Assign F and R to be the front and rear pointers of the queue and assign 0 to F and R.
- Queue Overflow: Before inserting a new element in to the Queue check whether Queue is full or not.
    - If REAR = N (ARRAYSIZE), Queue is full
- Queue Insertion: Get the new element Y to be inserted in to the queue
- If R is less than N, insert Y at the end, by incrementing R by 1. Otherwise display queue is full.
    - REAR=REAR+1
    - Q(REAR)=ITEM
- If F is zero, then assign F to be 1.
- Queue Underflow: Before deleting an element from the Queue check whether    Queue is empty or not.
    - If REAR<FRONT, Queue is empty
- Queue Deletion: To delete an element check whether F is greater than zero, then delete an element pointed by F, otherwise display queue is empty.
    - If F and R are equal the set F = R=0; otherwise F=F+1;
    - Display the queue Q from F to R.

### Program for Queue Implementation Using Arrays

```c
#include<stdio.h>
#define max 5
int q[max],front=-1,rear=-1,temp,e;
void enqueue()
{
  if(rear==(max-1))      //if(rear>max-1)
  {
    printf("queue is full");
  }
  else
  {
```

```c
        if(front==-1)
         {
            front=0;
         }
            scanf("%d",&e);
            rear=rear+1;
            q[rear]=e;
         }
}
void dequeue()
{
   if((front==-1)||(front==(rear+1)))
      {
      printf("queue is empty");
      }
   else
      {
         temp=q[front];
         front=front+1;
         printf("%d",temp);
      }
}
void display()
{int i;
   for( i=front;i<=rear;i++)
   {
      printf("%d",q[i]);
   }
}
int main()
{
   int choice;
   while(1)
   {
```

```
    printf("1.enqueue\n2.dequeue\n3.display");
    printf("enter the choice");
    scanf("%d",&choice);
    switch(choice)
    {
      case 1:enqueue();
      break;
      case 2:dequeue();
      break;
      case 3:display();
      break;
      case 4:exit(0);
      break;
    }
    }
    getch();
  }
```

### Analysis of Queue

- Enqueue : O(1)
- Dequeue : O(1)
- Size : O(1)

## 3.7.  Circular Queue

Circular queue is a linear data structure. It follows FIFO principle. In circular queue the last node is connected back to the first node to make a circle. Circular linked list fallow the First In First Out principle(FIFO).

Elements are added at the rear end and the elements are deleted at front end of the queue. It is also called as Wrap around queue or Ring buffer. Items can inserted and deleted from a queue in O(1) time. The main advantage of circular queue is memory utilization.

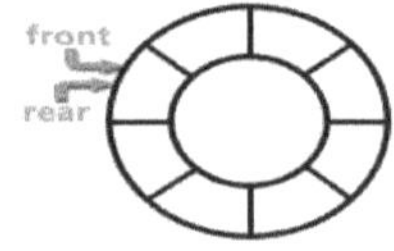

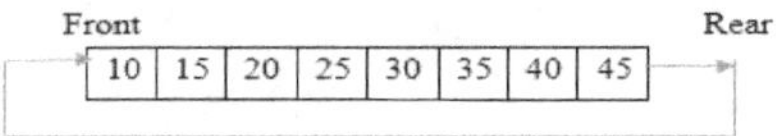



## *Initial Condition*

front=-1, rear=-1, size=0, max=5

## *Enqueue Condition*

```
if(front==-1)
{
        front=0;
}
if(max==size))
{
    printf("queue is full");
}
else
{
scanf("%d",&e);
rear=(raer+1)%max;
q[rear]=e;
Size++;
}
```

## *Dequeue Condition*

```
if(size==0)
{
printf("queue is empty");
}
else
{
temp=q[front];
front=(front+1)%max;
printf("%d",temp);
size--;
}
```

### *Display Function*

```
if(size==0)
{
Printf("queue is empty");
}
else
{
for(i=front;i!rear;i=(i+1)%max)
Printf("%d",q[i]);
}
Printf("%d",q[i]);
```

## 3.8.   Implementation of Queue Using Linked List

A queue data structure can be implemented using linked list data structure. The queue which is implemented using linked list can work for unlimited number of values. In linked list implementation of a queue, the last inserted node is always pointed by 'rear' and the first node is always pointed by 'front'.

### *Procedure*

- Create a singly linked list.
- Insertion Operation: Create a new node i.e., head and allocate space in memory
    - Check whether node is created or not
    - if node is created, get the value for the node and set the next field to NULL

        head->data=Value

        head->next=NULL
    - Check whether the queue is empty

        If (front==NULL and rear ==NULL)

        front =head

        rear= head
    - else [if queue is not empty]

        rear=head

        rear->next=head
- Deletion Operation: Create a temporary pointer,
    - Check whether the queue is empty , if not

- head=front
- Move front pointer to the next node adjacent to the deleted node
  Set front=head->Next
  Release memory i.e., free(head)
- To display the queue contents, traverse the list from the header till the last node.

## Program for Queue Using Linked List

```c
#include<stdio.h>
struct node
{
  int data;
  struct node *next;
}*front=NULL,*rear=NULL,*head;
void enqueue()
{
  int e;
  printf("\nenter elemnet");
  scanf("%d",&e);
  head=malloc(sizeof(struct node));
  head->data=e;
  head->next=NULL;
  if(front==NULL)
{
    front=head;
}
    rear->next=head;
    rear=head;
}
void dequeue()
{
if(front==NULL)
{
    printf("\nqueue is empty");
}
head=front;
```

```c
printf("%d",front->data);
front=front->next;
free(head);
}
void display()
{
 if(front==NULL)
{
    printf("queue is empty");
}
else
{
    head=front;
    while(head!=NULL)
{
     printf("%d",head->data);
     head=head->next;
}}
}int main()
{
  int ch;
  rear=malloc(sizeof(struct node));
  while(1)
  {
    printf("\n1.enqueue\n2.dequeue\n3.display\n4.exit");
    printf("\nenter your choice");
    scanf("%d",&ch);
    switch(ch)
    {
      case 1:enqueue();
      break;
      case 2:dequeue();
      break;
      case 3:display();
```

```
    break;
case 4:exit(0);
    break;
} } }
```

## 3.9.    Double Ended Queue

A Deque or deck is a double-ended queue. It allows elements to be added or removed on either the ends. It is also often called a head-tail linked list.

### *Types of Deque*

- An input-restricted deque is one where deletion can be made from both ends, but insertion can be made at one end only.
- An output-restricted deque is one where insertion can be made at both ends, but deletion can be made from one end only.

### *Deque as Stack and Queue*

- As Stack: Insertion and Deletion is made at the same time.
- As Queue: Items are inserted at one end and removed at another end.

### *Operations in Deque*

- Insert element at front
- Insert element at back
- Remove element at front
- Remove element at back
- Empty: It is used to test whether the deque is empty or not.

### *1.   Insert Element at Front*

Insert front is an operation used to push an element into the front of deque.

### *Algorithm for Insert Front*

Step 1: start

Step 2: check the queue is full or not as if (r==max-1)&& (f==0)

Step 3: if false update the pointer f as f =f-1

Step 4: Insert the element as pointer f as Q[f]=element.

Step 5: stop.

## 2. *Insert Element at Back*

Inert back is an operation used to push an element at the back of a deque

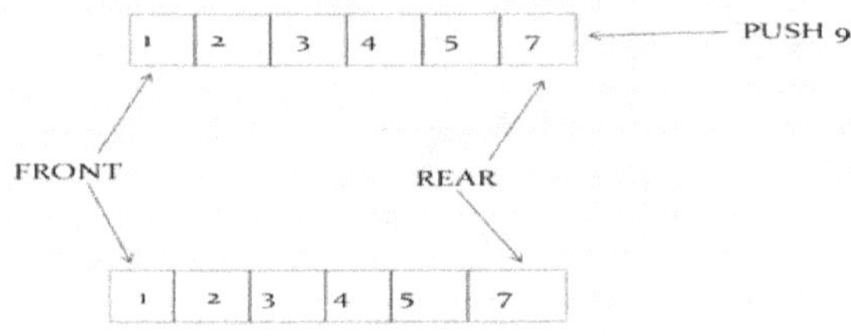


### *Algorithm for Insert back*

Step 1: start

Step 2: check the queue is full or not as if (r==max-1)

Step 3: If false update the pointer r as r=r+1

Step 4: Insert the element at pointer r as Q[r]=element

Step 5: stop

## 3. *Remove Element at Front*

Remove front is an operation used to pop an element on front of the deque.

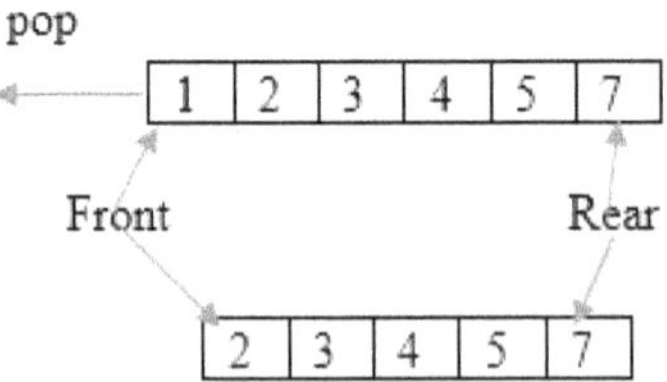

### *Algorithm for Remove Front*

Step 1: start

Step 2: check the queue is empty or not as if (f==r) if yes queue is empty

Step 3: if false update pointer f as f=f+1 and delete element at position f as element =Q[f]

Step 4: if (f==r) reset pointer f and r as f=r=-1

Step 5: stop

### 4. *Remove Element at Back*

Remove back is an operation used to pop an element at the back of the deque.

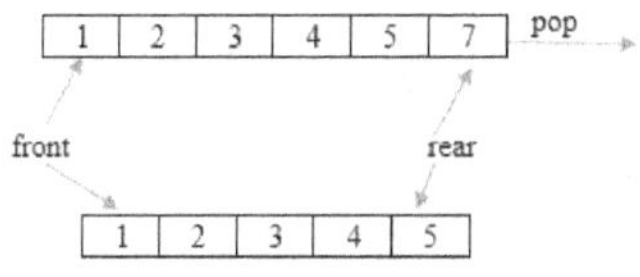

### *Algorithm Remove Back*

Step 1: start

Step 2: check the queue is empty or not as if (f==r) if yes queue is empty

Step 3: if false delete element at pointer r as element =Q[r]

Step 4: update pointer r as r=r-1

Step 5: if (f==r) reset pointer f and r as f=r=-1

Step 5: stop.

### *Application of Deque*

### *a. Palindrome-checker*

A palindromeis a string that reads the same forward and backward, for example, radar, toot, and madam. The solution to this problem will use a deque to store the characters of the string. We will process the string from left to right and add each character to the rear of the deque. At this point, the deque will be acting very much like an ordinary queue. The front of the deque will hold the first character of the string and the rear of the deque will hold the last character.

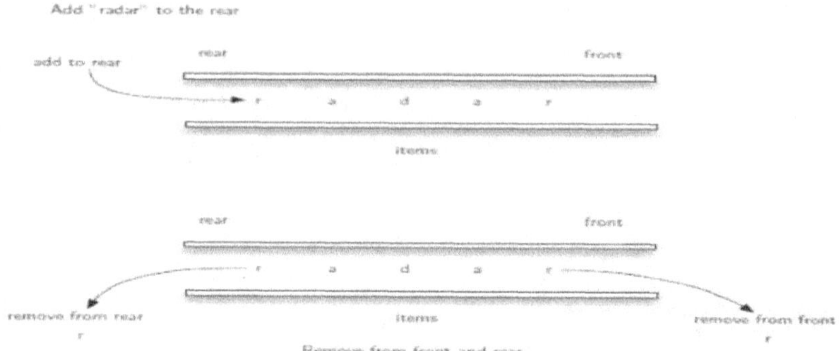



### b. A-steal Job Scheduling Algorithm

The A-Steal job scheduling algorithm implement task scheduling for several processors

The processor gets the first element from the deque.

When one of the processor completes execution of its own threads it can steal a thread from another processor.

It gets the last element from the deque of another processor and executes it.

## 3.10. Priority Queue

The Priority Queue ADT has the same interface as the Queue ADT, but different semantics. The semantic difference is that the item that is removed from the queue is not necessarily the first one that was added. Rather, it is whatever item in the queue has the highest priority. If two elements have the same priority, they are served according to their order in the queue.

### Operation in Priority Queue

1. Insertion: same as normal queue(Enqueue)
2. Deletion: It finds the current minimum element in the queue, deletes it from the queue, and returns it.

# CHAPTER 4

# TREES

## 4.1. Introduction

Tree is a non-linear data structure which organizes data in hierarchical structure and it is defined as collection of nodes.

In tree data structure, every individual element is called as Node. Node in a tree data structure, stores the actual data of that particular element and link to next element in hierarchical structure. Tree consists of distinguished node r, root and zero or more nonempty subtrees $T_1, T_2, T_3, \ldots T_K$

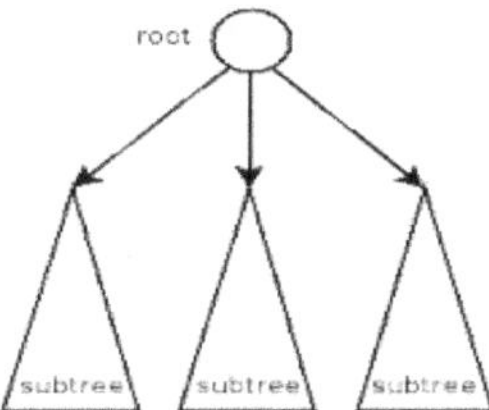


### *Recursive Definition*

Tree is a collection of N nodes, one is root and N-1 edges.

Each edge connects some node to its parent and every node except the root has one parent.

## 4.2. Terminology in Trees

### *1. Root*

In a tree data structure, the first node is called as Root Node. Every tree must have root node. We can say that root node is the origin of tree data structure. In any tree, there must be only one root node. We never have multiple root nodes in a tree.

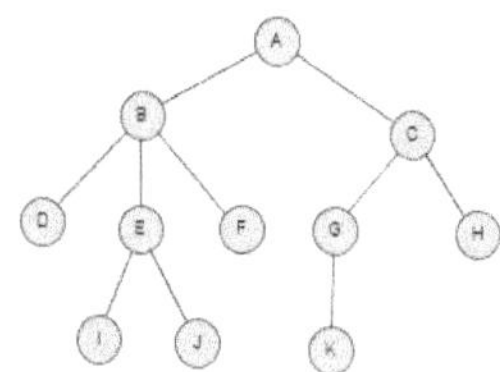


A → Root Node

First Node is the Root Node for every tree

## 2. *Edge*

In a tree data structure, the connecting link between any two nodes is called as edge. In a tree with 'N' number of nodes there will be a maximum of 'N-1' number of edges.

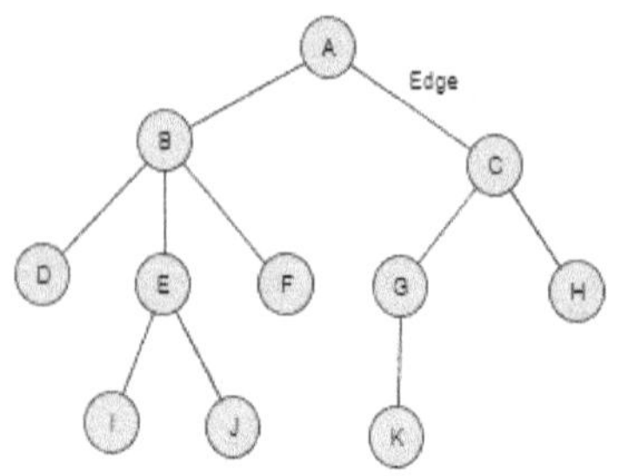


In every tree, Edge is a connecting link between two nodes

## 3. *Parent*

In a tree data structure, the node which is predecessor of any node is called as PARENT NODE. In simple words, the node which has branch from it to any other node is called as parent node. Parent node can also be defined as "The node which has child / children".

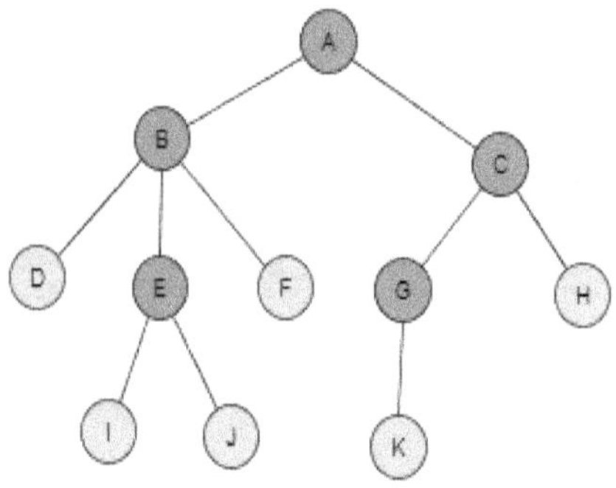


A, B,C,E & G are parent nodes

## 4. *Child*

In a tree data structure, the node which is descendant of any node is called as CHILD Node. In simple words, the node which has a link from its parent node is called as child node. In a tree, any parent node can have any number of child nodes. In a tree, all the nodes except root are child nodes.

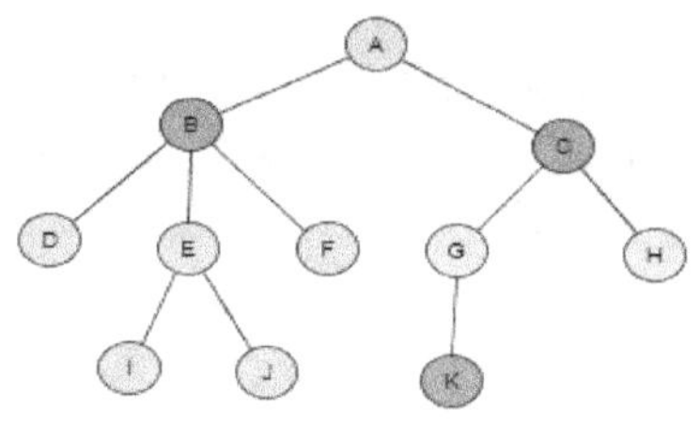

B & C are Children of A

G & H are Children of C

K is Child of G

Descendant of any node is child node

## 5. *Siblings*

In a tree data structure, nodes which belong to same Parent are called as SIBLINGS. In simple words, the nodes with same parent are called as Sibling nodes.

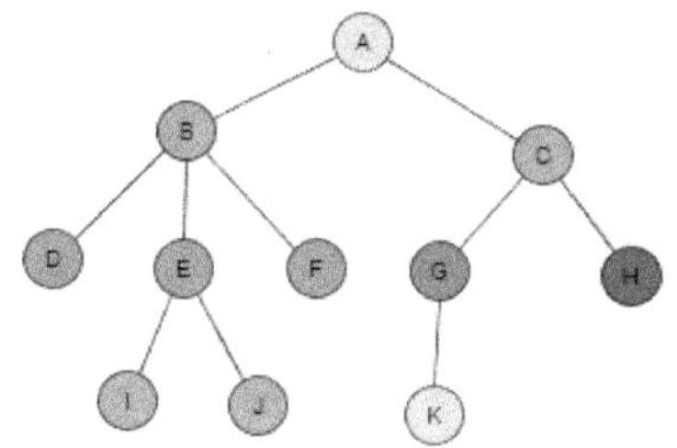

B C are Siblings

D E F are Siblings

G H are Siblings

I J are Siblings

## 6. *Leaf*

In a tree data structure, the node which does not have a child is called as LEAF Node. In simple words, a leaf is a node with no child. In a tree data structure, the leaf nodes are also called as External Nodes. External node is also a node with no child. In a tree, leaf node is also called as 'Terminal' node.

D, I, J, F, K & H are leaf nodes

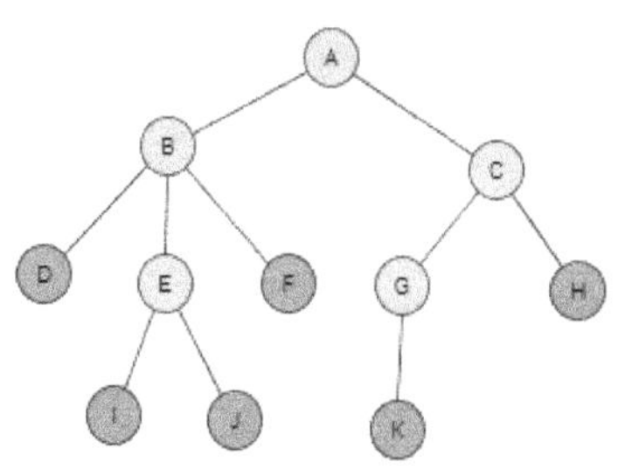

## 7. *Internal Nodes*

In a tree data structure, the node which has atleast one child is called as INTERNAL Node. In simple words, an internal node is a node with atleast one child. In a tree data structure, nodes other than leaf nodes are called as Internal Nodes. The root node is also said to be Internal Node if the tree has more than one node. Internal nodes are also called as 'Non-Terminal' nodes.

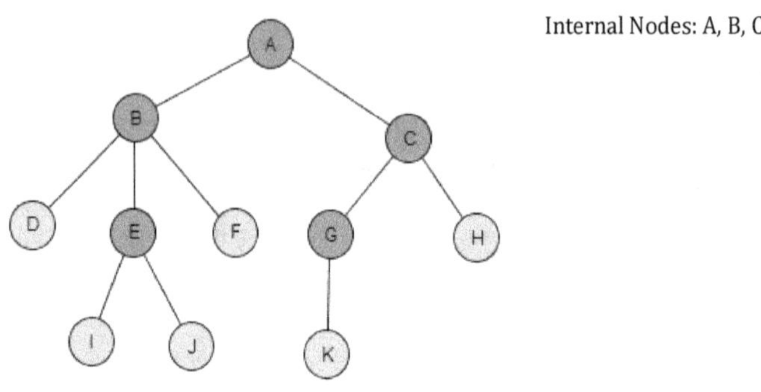

Internal Nodes: A, B, C, E & G

## 8. *Degree*

In a tree data structure, the total number of children of a node is called as DEGREE of that Node. In simple words, the Degree of a node is total number of children it has. The highest degree of a node among all the nodes in a tree is called as 'Degree of Tree'

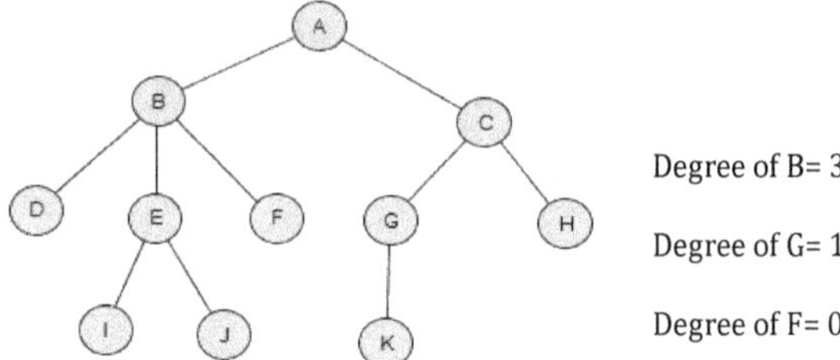

Degree of B= 3

Degree of G= 1

Degree of F= 0

## 9. *Level*

In a tree data structure, the root node is said to be at Level 0 and the children of root node are at Level 1 and the children of the nodes which are at Level 1 will be at Level 2 and so on... In simple words, in a tree each step from top to bottom is called as a Level and the Level count starts with '0' and incremented by one at each level (Step).

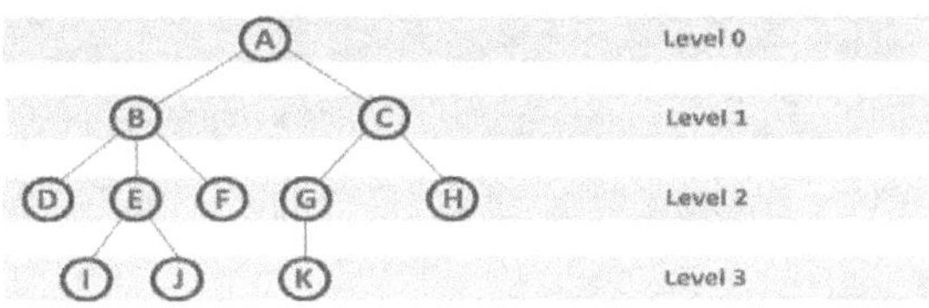


## 10. Height

In a tree data structure, the total number of edges from leaf node to a particular node in the longest path is called as HEIGHT of that Node. In a tree, height of the root node is said to be height of the tree. In a tree, height of all leaf nodes is '0'.

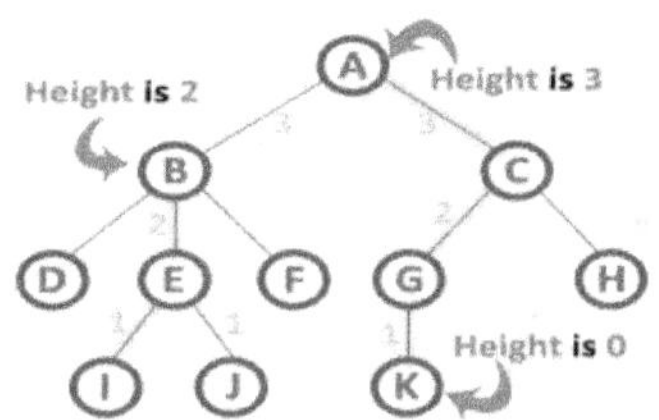


Height of Tree = 3

## 11. Depth

In a tree data structure, the total number of edges from root node to a particular node is called as DEPTH of that Node. In a tree, the total number of edges from root node to a leaf node in the longest path is said to be Depth of the tree. In simple words, the highest depth of any leaf node in a tree is said to be depth of that tree. In a tree, depth of the root node is '0'.

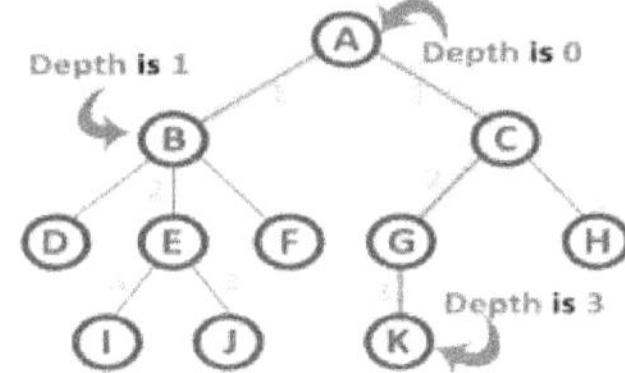


Depth of the Tree = 3

## 12. Path

In a tree data structure, the sequence of Nodes and Edges from one node to another node is called as PATH between that two Nodes. Length of a Path is total number of nodes in that path. In below example the path A - B - E - J has length 4.

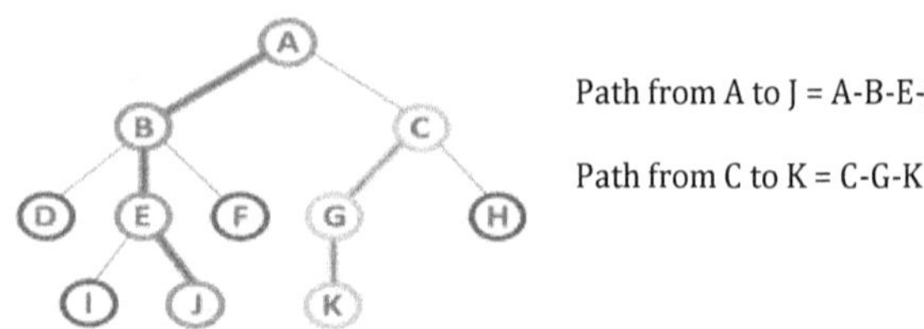

Path from A to J = A-B-E-J

Path from C to K = C-G-K

## 13. Sub Tree

In a tree data structure, each child from a node forms a subtree recursively. Every child node will form a subtree on its parent node.

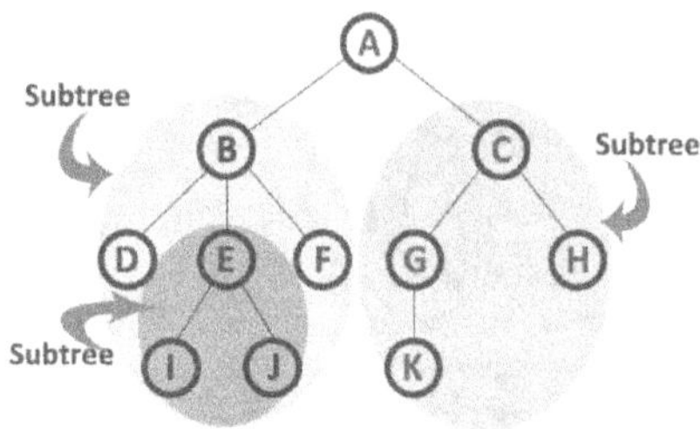


### *Example*

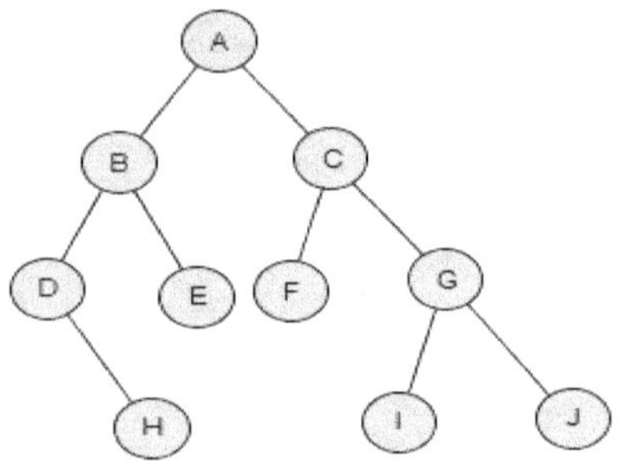

For Leaf Node height, will be always 0

Height of the tree=3

Height of the root=3

Depth of the tree =3

| Node | Height | Depth/Level |
|------|--------|-------------|
| A | 3 | 0 |
| B | 2 | 1 |
| C | 2 | 1 |
| D | 1 | 2 |
| E | 0 | 2 |
| F | 0 | 2 |
| G | 1 | 2 |
| H | 0 | 3 |
| I | 0 | 3 |
| J | 0 | 3 |

## 4.3.  Implementation of Trees

### *First child/Next Siblings Representation of Trees*

In this representation, we use list with one type of node which consists of three fields namely Data field, Left child reference field and Right sibling reference field. Data field stores the actual value of a node, left reference field stores the address of the left child and right reference field stores the address of the right sibling node. Graphical representation of that node is as follows.

| Data | |
|------|------|
| First child | Next Siblings |

In this representation, every node's data field stores the actual value of that node. If that node has left child, then left reference field stores the address of that left child node otherwise that field stores NULL. If that node has right sibling, then right reference field stores the address of right sibling node otherwise that field stores NULL. The tree example can be represented using First child/Next Siblings representation as follows.

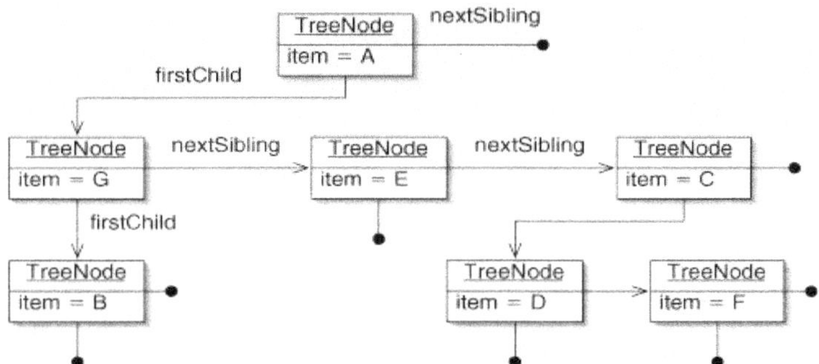

### *Structure Definition*

```
struct TreeNode
{
int data;
struct TreeNode * Firstchild;
struct TreeNode *Nextsibilings;
}
```

## 4.4.  Binary Tree

A binary tree is a tree in which no node can have more than two children. It consists of root and two sub trees $T_L$ and $T_R$.

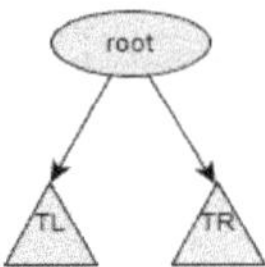


## 4.5.  Types of Binary Tree

### 1.  *Complete Binary Tree*

A complete binary tree is a binary tree in which every level, except possibly the last, is completely filled, and all nodes are as far left as possible. Complete binary tree is also called as Perfect Binary Tree.

Complete but not full binary tree

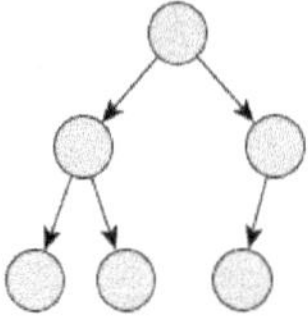

In a tree of height h

- Leaves are at level h
- Number of leaves is $2^h$
- Number of internal nodes=$1+2+2^2+.....+2^h-1$=Number of leaves-1
- Total number of nodes is $2^{h+1}-1$=n

In a tree of n nodes

- Number of leaves is (n+1)/2

- Height =$\log_2$

## 2. *Full Binary Tree*

A binary tree T is full if each node is either a leaf or possesses exactly two child nodes. A binary tree in which every node has either two or zero number of children is called Full Binary Tree. Full binary tree data structure is used to represent mathematical expressions. Full binary tree is also called as Strictly Binary Tree or Proper Binary Tree or 2-Tree.

Full but not complete binary Tree

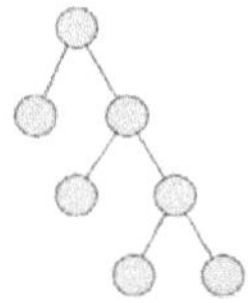

Neither Complete nor full    Full and Complete

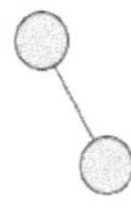 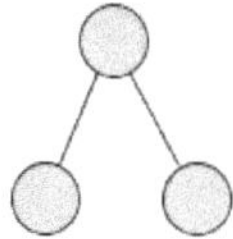

## 3. *Extended Binary Tree*

The full binary tree obtained by adding dummy nodes to a binary tree is called as Extended Binary Tree.

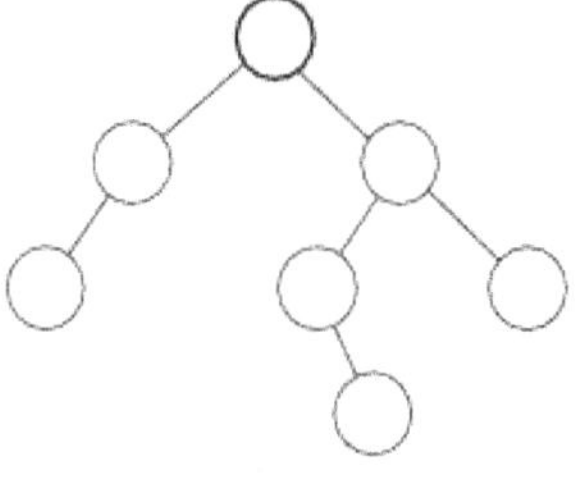 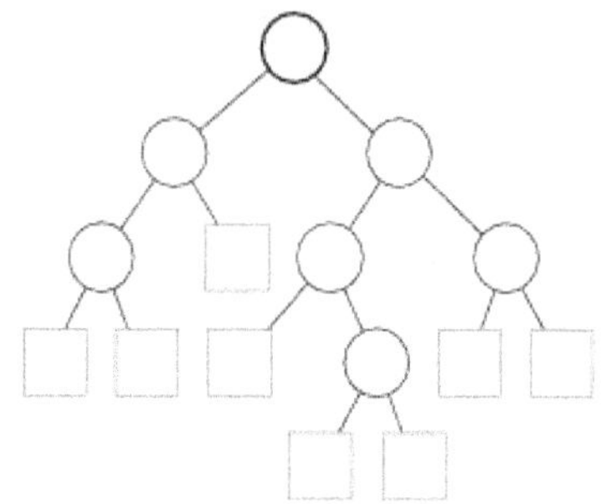

## 4.6.  Binary Tree Representation

A binary tree data structure is represented using two methods. Those methods are as follows.

- Array Representation
- Linked List Representation

Consider the following binary tree.

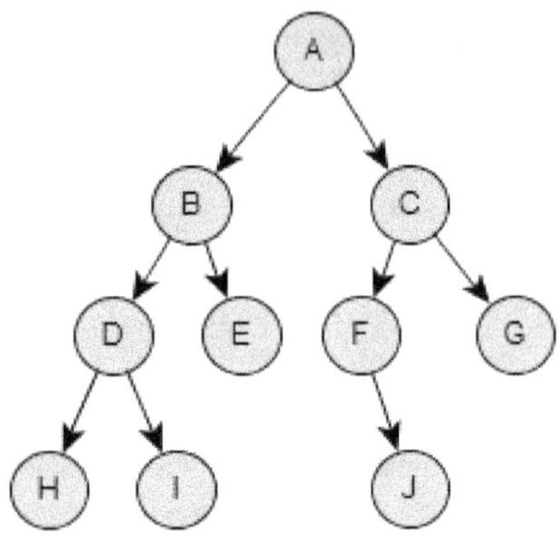

### 1.  Array Representation

In array representation of binary tree, we use a one-dimensional array (1-D Array) to represent a binary tree.To represent a binary tree of depth 'n' using array representation, we need one dimensional array with a maximum size of $2^{n+1} - 1$.

| A | B | C | D | E | F | G | H | I | - | - | - | J | - | - | - | - | - | - | - | - | - | - |
|---|---|---|---|---|---|---|---|---|---|---|---|---|---|---|---|---|---|---|---|---|---|---|

### 2.  Linked List Representation

We use double linked list to represent a binary tree. In a double linked list, every node consists of three fields.

- First field for storing left child address,
- Second for storing actual data and
- Third for storing right child address.

In this linked list representation, a node has the following structure

| Left Child Address | Data | Right Child Address |
|---|---|---|

The above example of binary tree represented using Linked list representation is shown as follows

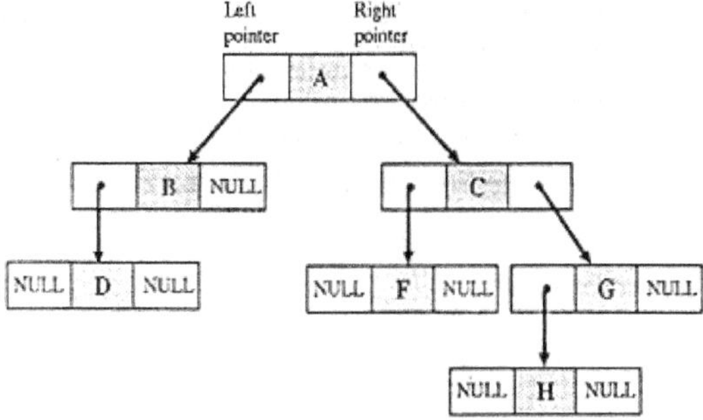


## 4.7.    Expression Tree

A special kind of binary tree in which:

1.    Each leaf node contains a single operand
2.    Each nonleaf node contains a single binary operator
3.    The left and right subtrees of an operator node represent subexpressions that must be evaluated before applying the operator at the root of the subtree.

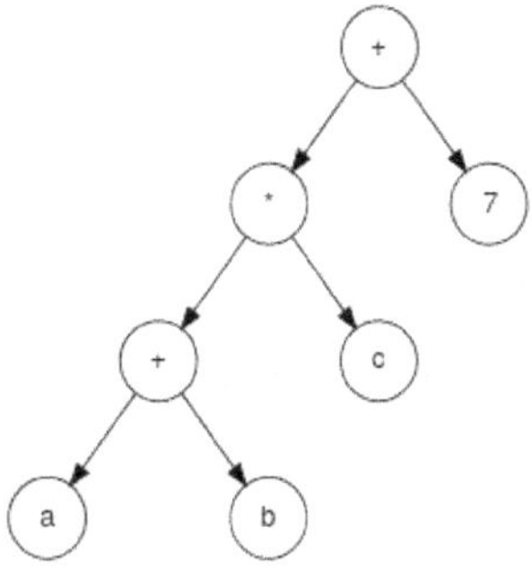


### *Construction of Expression Tree*

The evaluation of the tree takes place by reading the postfix expression one symbol at a time. If the symbol is an operand, one-node tree is created and a pointer is pushed onto a stack. If the symbol is an operator, the pointers are popped to two trees T1 and T2 from the stack and a new tree whose root is the operator and whose left and right children point to T2 and T1 respectively is formed . A pointer to this new tree is then pushed to the Stack.

## *Example*

The input is: **a b + c d e + * ***

Since the first two symbols are operands, one-node trees are created and pointers are pushed to them onto a stack. For convenience, the stack will grow from left to right.

Stack growing from left to right

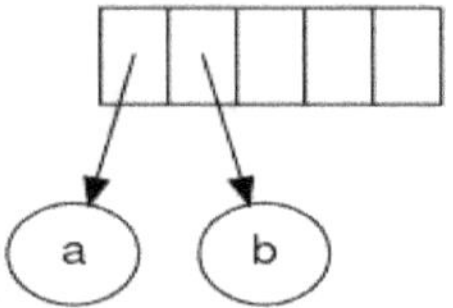

The next symbol is a '+'. It pops the two pointers to the trees, a new tree is formed, and a pointer to it is pushed onto to the stack.

Formation of a new tree

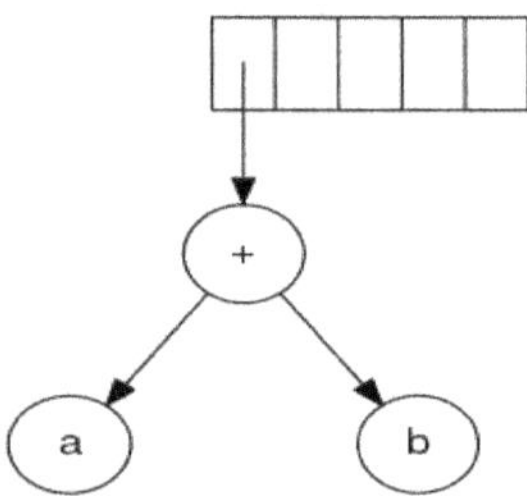

Next, c, d, and e are read. A one-node tree is created for each and a pointer to the corresponding tree is pushed onto the stack.

Creating a one-node tree

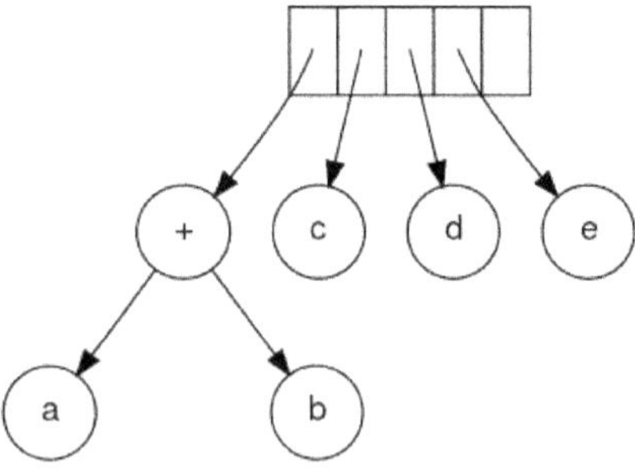

Continuing, a '+' is read, and it merges the last two trees.

Merging two trees

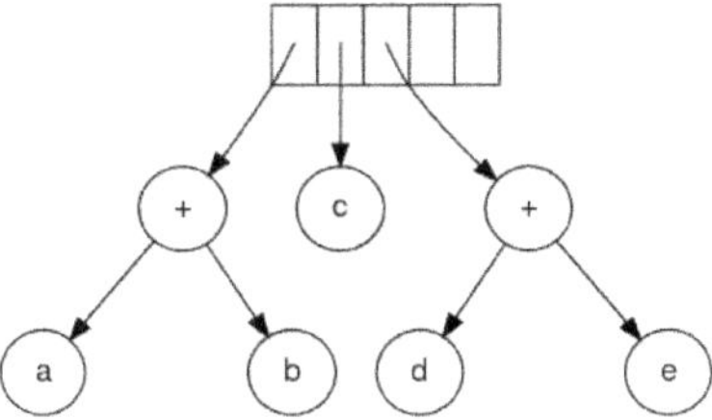

Now, a '*' is read. The last two tree pointers are popped and a new tree is formed with a '*' as the root.

Forming a new tree with a root

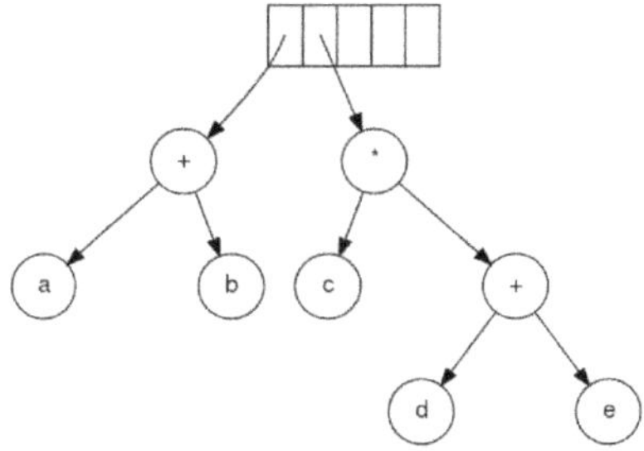

Finally, the last symbol is read. The two trees are merged and a pointer to the final tree remains on the stack.

Steps to construct an expression tree a b + c d e + * *

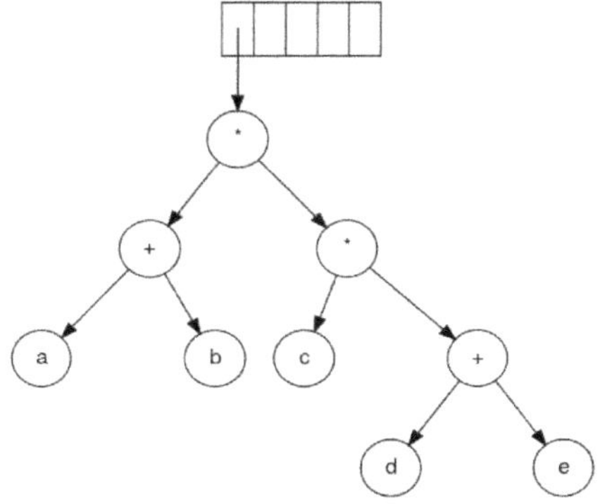

## *Program to Implement Expression Tree Using Stacks find its In-order, Pre-order & Post-order Traversals Using C Language*

```c
#include<stdio.h>
#include<conio.h>
#include<malloc.h>
typedef struct tree
{
char data;
struct tree *left;
struct tree *right;
}*pos;
pos stack[30];
int top=-1;
pos newnode(char b)
{
pos temp;
temp=(struct tree*)malloc(sizeof(struct tree));
temp->data=b;
temp->left=NULL;
temp->right=NULL;
return(temp);
}
void push(pos temp)
{
stack[++top]=temp;
}
pos pop()
{
pos p;
p=stack[top--];
return(p);
}
void inorder(pos t)
{
```

```c
if(t!=NULL)
{
inorder(t->left);
printf("%s",t->data);
inorder(t->right);
}
}
void preorder(pos t)
{
if(t!=NULL)
{
printf("%s",t->data);
preorder(t->left);
inorder(t->right);
}
}
void postorder(pos t)
{
if(t!=NULL)
{
postorder(t->left);
postorder(t->right);
printf("%s",t->data);
}
}
void main()
{
char a[20];pos temp,t;int j,i;
clrscr();
printf("\nEnter the postfix expression");
gets(a);
for(i=0;a[i]!=NULL;i++)
{
if(a[i]=='*' || a[i]=='/' || a[i]=='+' || a[i]=='-')
```

```
{
temp=newnode(a[i]);
temp->right=pop();
temp->left=pop();
push(temp);
}
else
{
temp=newnode(a[i]);
push(temp);
}
}
inorder(temp);
printf("\n");
preorder(temp);
printf("\n");
postorder(temp);
getch();
}
```

## 4.8.    Binary Search Tree

A Binary Search Tree (BST) is a tree in which all the nodes follow the properties.

- The left sub-tree of a node has a key less than or equal to its parent node's key.
- The right sub-tree of a node has a key greater than or equal to its parent node's key.

$$\text{left\_subtree (keys)} \leq \text{node (key)} \leq \text{right\_subtree (keys)}$$

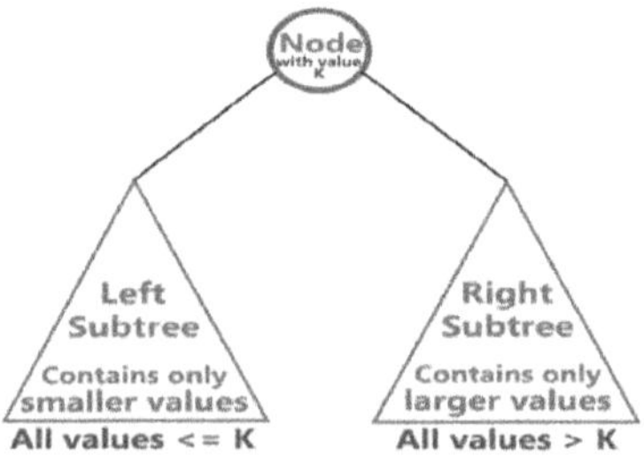

A binary tree has the following time complexities.

- Search Operation - O(n)
- Insertion Operation - O(1)
- Deletion Operation - O(n)

## Structure Definition

struct node

{

    int element;

    struct node*left;

    struct node*right;

};

## Basic Operations

## Search Operation

In a binary search tree, the search operation is performed with **O(log n)** time complexity.

## Algorithm

Step 1: Read the search element from the user

Step 2: Compare, the search element with the value of root node in the tree.

Step 3: If both are matching, then display "Given node found!!!" and terminate the function

Step 4: If both are not matching, then check whether search element is smaller or larger than that node value.

Step 5: If search element is smaller, then continue the search process in left subtree.

Step 6: If search element is larger, then continue the search process in right subtree.

Step 7: Repeat the same until we found exact element or we completed with a leaf node

Step 8: If we reach to the node with search value, then display "Element is found" and terminate the function.

Step 9: If we reach to a leaf node and it is also not matching, then display "Element not found" and terminate the function.

### *Routine*

```
tree find (int x,tree t)
{
   if(t==NULL)
      return NULL;
   if(x>t->element)
      return find(x,t->right);
      else
      if(x<t->element)
      return find(x,t->left);
      else
      return(t);
}
```

### *Insertion Operation*

Whenever an element is to be inserted, first locate its proper location. Start searching from the root node, then if the data is less than the key value, search for the empty location in the left subtree and insert the data. Otherwise, search for the empty location in the right subtree and insert the data.

In a binary search tree, the insertion operation is performed with O(log n) time complexity. In binary search tree, new node is always inserted as a leaf node.

### *Algorithm*

**Step 1:** Create a newNode with given value and set its left and right to NULL.

**Step 2:** Check whether tree is Empty.

**Step 3:** If the tree is Empty, then set root to newNode.

**Step 4:** If the tree is Not Empty, then check whether value of newNode is smaller or largerthan the node (here it is root node).

**Step 5:** If newNode is smaller than or equalto the node, then move to its left child. If newNode is largerthan the node, then move to its rightchild.

**Step 6:** Repeat the above step until we reach to a leafnode (i.e., reach to NULL).

**Step 7:** After reaching a leaf node, then insert the newNode as left child if newNode is smaller or equal to that leaf else insert it as right child.

### *Routine*

```
tree insert(int x,tree t)
{
   if(t==NULL)
   {
      t=malloc(sizeof(struct node));
      t->element=x;
      t->left=NULL;
      t->right=NULL;
   }
   else if(x>t->element)
      t->right=insert(x,t->right);
   else if(x<t->element)
      t->left=insert(x,t->left);
      return(t);
}
```

## *Deletion Operation*

In a binary search tree, the deletion operation is performed with O(log n) time complexity. Deleting a node from Binary search tree has following three cases.

**Case 1:** Deleting a Leaf node (A node with no children)

**Case 2:** Deleting a node with one child

**Case 3:** Deleting a node with two children

## *Case 1: Deleting a Leaf Node (A Node with no Children)*

We use the following steps to delete a leaf node from BST.

**Step 1:**Findthe node to be deleted using search operation

**Step 2:** Delete the node using free function (If it is a leaf) and terminate the function.

## *Case 2: Deleting a Node with One Child*

We use the following steps to delete a node with one child from BST.

**Step 1:**Findthe node to be deleted using search operation

**Step 2:** If it has only one child, then create a link between its parent and child nodes.

**Step 3:** Delete the node using free function and terminate the function.

## Case 3: Deleting a Node with Two Children

We use the following steps to delete a node with two children from BST.

**Step 1:**Find the node to be deleted using search operation

**Step 2:** If it has two children, then find the largestnode in itsleft subtree (OR) the smallestnode in its right subtree.

**Step 3:**Swapboth deleting node and node which found in above step.

**Step 4:** Then, check whether deleting node came to case 1orcase 2else goto steps 2

**Step 5:** If it comes to case 1, then delete using case 1 logic.

**Step 6:** If it comes to case 2, then delete using case 2 logic.

**Step 7:** Repeat the same process until node is deleted from the tree.

## Routine

```
tree del(int x,tree t)
{
  if(t==NULL)
    printf("Element not found");
  else if(x<t->element)
    t->left=del(x,t->left);
  else if(x>t->element)
    t->right=del(x,t->right);
  else if(t->left&&t->right)
  {
    temp=findmin(t->right);
    t->element=temp->element;
    t->right=del(t->element,t->right);
  }
  else
  {
    temp=t;
    if(t->left==NULL)
      t=t->right;
```

```
   else if(t->right==NULL)
     t=t->left;
   free(temp);
  }
  return t;
}
```

## Example 1

Construct a Binary Search Tree by inserting the following sequence of numbers. 10,12,5,4,20,8,7,15 and 13

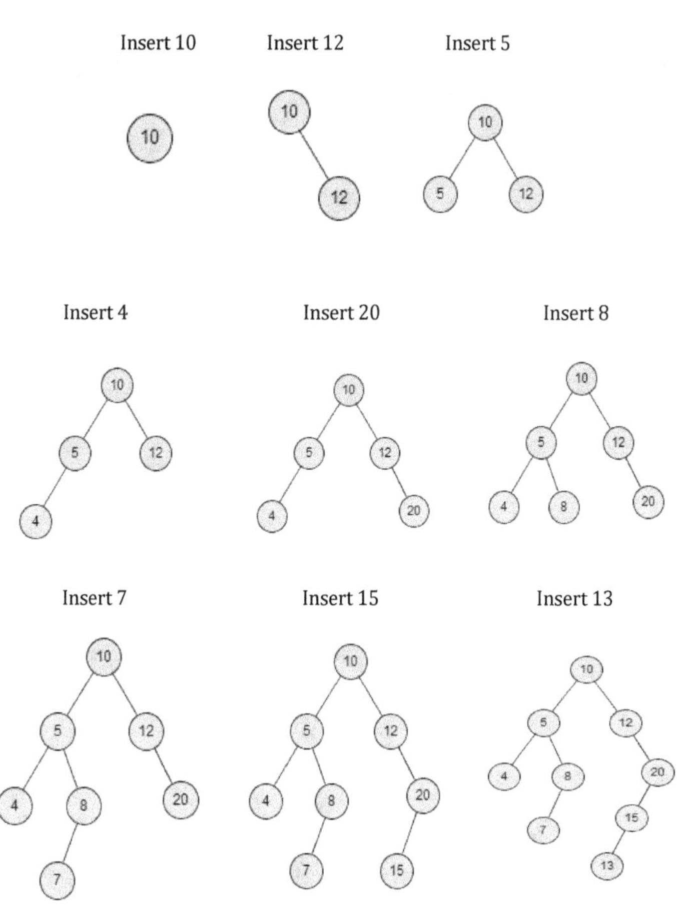

## *Example 2*

Draw the binary Search tree which would be created by inserting the following numbers in the order given 50   30   25   75   82   32   63

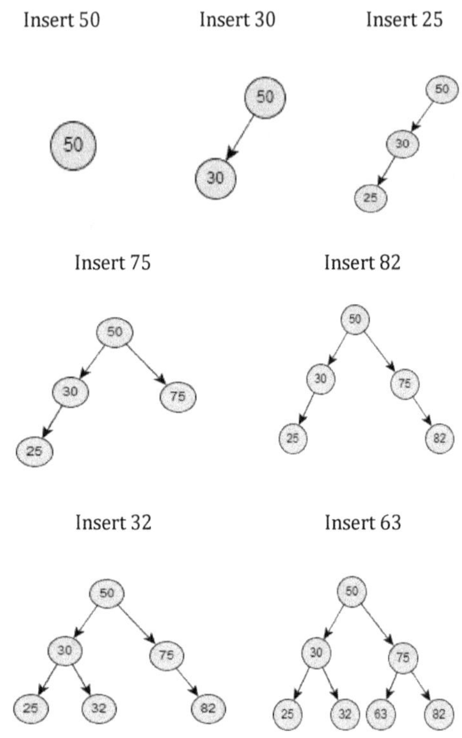



Delete 30 from the BST

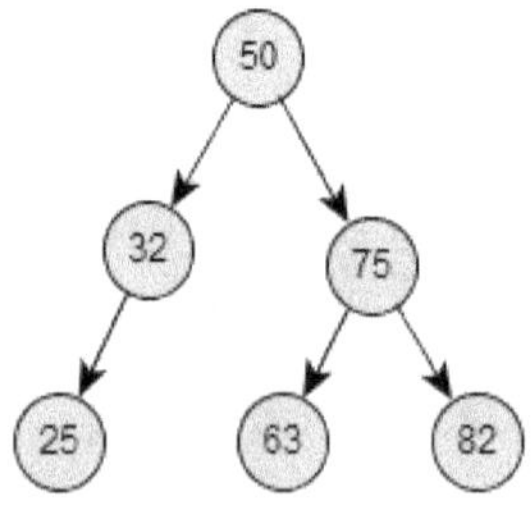

### Program for Binary Search Tree

```c
#include<stdio.h>
struct node
{
   int element;
   struct node*left;
   struct node*right;
};
typedef struct node*tree;
tree t=NULL,temp;
tree insert(int x,tree t)
{
  if(t==NULL)
  {
     t=malloc(sizeof(struct node));
     t->element=x;
     t->left=NULL;
     t->right=NULL;
  }
  else if(x>t->element)
     t->right=insert(x,t->right);
  else if(x<t->element)
     t->left=insert(x,t->left);
     return(t);
}
tree find (int x,tree t)
{
  if(t==NULL)
     return NULL;
  if(x>t->element)
     return find(x,t->right);
     else
     if(x<t->element)
     return find(x,t->left);
```

```c
      else
      return(t);
}
tree findmin(tree t)
{
  if(t==NULL)
     return NULL;
  if(t->left==NULL)
     return(t);
  else
     return findmin(t->left);
}
tree findmax(tree t)
{
  if(t==NULL)
     return NULL;
  if(t->right==NULL)
     return(t);
  else
     return findmax(t->right);
}
tree del(int x,tree t)
{
  if(t==NULL)
     printf("Element not found");
  else if(x<t->element)
     t->left=del(x,t->left);
  else if(x>t->element)
     t->right=del(x,t->right);
  else if(t->left&&t->right)
  {
     temp=findmin(t->right);
     t->element=temp->element;
     t->right=del(t->element,t->right);
```

```c
    }
    else
    {
     temp=t;
     if(t->left==NULL)
       t=t->right;
     else if(t->right==NULL)
       t=t->left;
     free(temp);
    }
    return t;
}
void in(tree t)
{
   if(t!=NULL)
   {
      in(t->left);
      printf("\t%d,",t->element);
      in(t->right);
   }
}
void post(tree t)
{
   if(t!=NULL)
   {
      post(t->left);
      post(t->right);
      printf("\t%d",t->element);
   }
}
void pre(tree t)
{
   if(t!=NULL)
   {
```

```c
    printf("\t%d",t->element);
    pre(t->left);
    pre(t->right);
  }
}
int main()
{
  int ch,n,a;
  while(1)
  {
  printf("\n1.insertion\n2.delete\n3.find\n4.min\n5.max\n6.inorder post preorder\n7.exit");
  printf("\nenter the choice");
  scanf("%d",&ch);
  switch(ch)
  {case 1:
      printf("\nEnter the element to be inserted");
      scanf("%d",&n);
      t=insert(n,t);
      break;
    case 2:
      printf("\nEnter the element to be deleted");
      scanf("%d",&n);
      t=del(n,t);
      break;
    case 3:
      printf("\nEnter the element to be found");
      scanf("%d",&n);
      temp=find(n,t);
      if(temp!=NULL)
        printf("Element found");
      else
        printf("Element not found");
      break;
```

```c
        case 4:
          temp=findmin(t);
          printf("\n%d is the minimum element",temp->element);
          break;
        case 5:
          temp=findmax(t);
          printf("\n%d is the maximum element",temp->element);
          break;
        case 6:
          printf("\n1.Inorder\n2.Postorder\n3.Preorder\nEnter your choice...");
          printf("enter your choice");
          scanf("%d",&a);
          switch(a)
          {
          case 1:
            in(t);
            break;
          case 2:
            post(t);
            break;
          case 3:
            pre(t);
            break;
          }
          break;
        case 7:
          exit(0);
        }}
    }
```

## 4.9.    Threaded Binary Trees

A binary tree is represented using array representation or linked list representation. When a binary tree is represented using linked list representation, if any node is not having a child we use NULL pointer in that position.

In any binary tree linked list representation, there are more number of NULL pointer than actual pointers. Generally, in any binary tree linked list representation, if there are 2Nnumber of reference fields, then N+1 number of reference fields are filled with NULL ( N+1 are NULL out of 2N ).

This NULL pointer does not play any role except indicating there is no link (no child). A. J. Perlis and C. Thornton have proposed new binary tree called "Threaded Binary Tree", which make use of NULL pointer to improve its traversal processes.

In threaded binary tree, NULL pointers are replaced by references to other nodes in the tree, called threads.

Threaded Binary Tree is also a binary tree in which all left child pointers that are NULL (in Linked list representation) points to its in-order predecessor, and all right child pointers that are NULL (in Linked list representation) points to its in-order successor. If there is no in-order predecessor or in-order successor, then it point to root node.

Consider the following binary tree

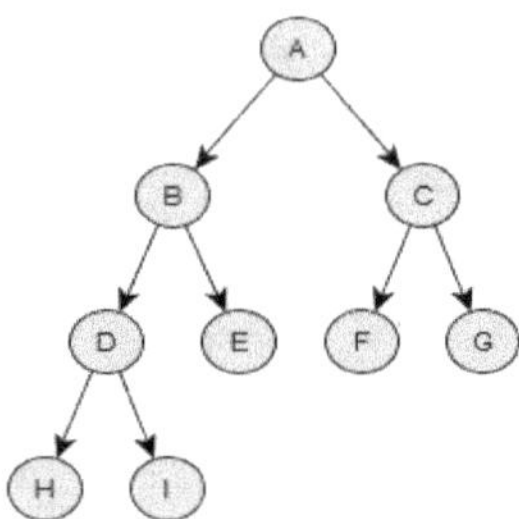

To convert above binary tree into threaded binary tree, first find the in-order traversal of that tree.

### In-order Traversal of above Binary Tree

**H-D-I-B-E-A-F-J-C-G**

When we represent above binary tree using linked list representation, nodes H, I, E, F, J and Gleft child pointers are NULL. This NULL is replaced by address of its in-order predecessor, respectively (I to D, E to B, F to A, J to F and G to C), but here the node H does not have its in-order predecessor, so it points to the root node A. And nodes H, I, E, J and Gright child pointers are NULL.

This NULL pointer is replaced by address of its in-order successor, respectively (H to D, I to B, E to A, and J to C), but here the node G does not have its in-order successor, so it points to the root node A.

Above example binary tree become as follows after converting into threaded binary tree

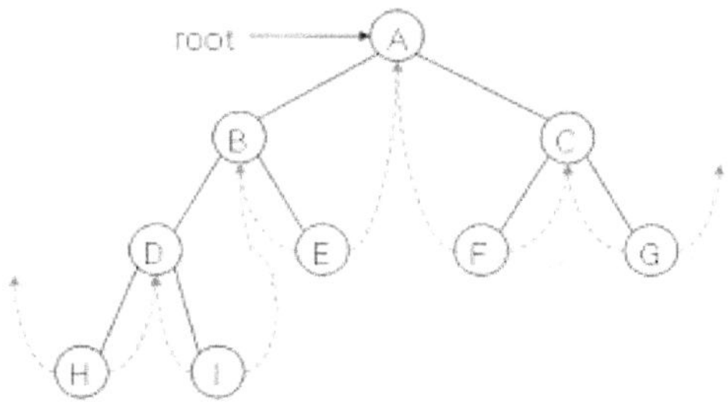

The threads are indicated with dotted links.

Though we can represent a thread link using dotted lines pictorially, to represent them implicitly, a separate Boolean flag is needed for each of the left and right pointers. The node structure in that case is shown in the fig, where lthread and rthread are Boolean indicators associated with the left and right links respectively. The following coding scheme is used to distinguish between a structural link and a thread.

lthread=true(1)-left thread link

lthread=false(0)-left structural link

rthread=true(1)-right thread link

lthread=false(0)-right structural link

| lptr | lthread | data | rthread | rptr |
|------|---------|------|---------|------|

A Node in a Threaded Binary Tree

The algorithm for inorder successor traversal of the node p.

**ins(p)**

1.  q= rchild(p)

    if (rthread(p)=0)

    then return (q)

2.  Repeat while rthread (q) = 0

    q= lchild (q)

3.  return (q)

The algorithm for inorder predecessor traversal of the node p.

inp (p)

1.  q= lchild(p)

    if (lthread(p)=0)

    then return (q)

2.  Repeat while lthread (q) = 0

    q= rchild (q)

3.  return (q)

## 4.10.  Binary Tree Traversals

Displaying (or) visiting order of nodes in a binary tree is called as Binary Tree Traversal. There are three types of binary tree traversals.

1.  In - Order Traversal

2.  Pre - Order Traversal

3.  Post - Order Traversal

Consider the following binary tree.

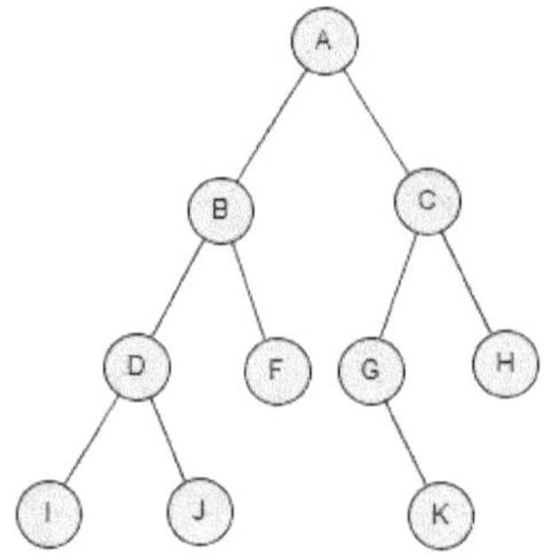


### 1.  *In-Order Traversal:( Left Child-Root-Right Child)*

In In-Order traversal, the root node is visited between left child and right child. In this traversal, the left child node is visited first, then the root node is visited and later we go for visiting right child node. This in-order traversal is applicable for every root node of all subtrees in the tree. This is performed recursively for all nodes in the tree.

In-Order Traversal: **I - D - J - B - F - A - G - K - C – H**

## 2. *Pre-Order Traversal (Root -Left Child-Right Child)*

In Pre-Order traversal, the root node is visited before left child and right child nodes. In this traversal, the root node is visited first, then its left child and later its right child. This pre-order traversal is applicable for every root node of all subtrees in the tree.

Pre - Order Traversal: **A-B-D-I-J-F-C-G-K-H**

## 3. *Post - Order Traversal (Left Child-Right Child-Root)*

In Post-Order traversal, the root node is visited after left child and right child.

In this traversal, left child node is visited first, then its right child and then its root node. This is recursively performed until the right most node is visited.

Post - Order Traversal: **I - J - D - F - B - K - G - H - C – A**

## *Program for Tree Traversal*

```c
#include <stdio.h>
#include <stdlib.h>
struct node
{
   int value;
   node* left;
   node* right;
};
struct node* root;
struct node* insert(struct node* r, int data);
void inOrder(struct node* r);
void preOrder(struct node* r);
void postOrder(struct node* r);
int main()
{
   root = NULL;
   int n, v;
   printf("How many data's do you want to insert ?\n");
   scanf("%d", &n);
   for(int i=0; i<n; i++){
   printf("Data %d: ", i+1);
```

```c
    scanf("%d", &v);
   root = insert(root, v);
}
   printf("Inorder Traversal: ");
   inOrder(root);
   printf("\n");
   printf("Preorder Traversal: ");
   preOrder(root);
   printf("\n");
   printf("Postorder Traversal: ");
   postOrder(root);
   printf("\n");
   return 0;
}
struct node* insert(struct node* r, int data)
{
   if(r==NULL)
   {
      r = (struct node*) malloc(sizeof(struct node));
      r->value = data;
      r->left = NULL;
      r->right = NULL;
   }
   else if(data < r->value){
      r->left = insert(r->left, data);
   }
   else {
      r->right = insert(r->right, data);
   }
   return r;
}
void inOrder(struct node* r)
{
   if(r!=NULL){
```

```
      inOrder(r->left);
      printf("%d ", r->value);
      inOrder(r->right);
   }
}
void preOrder(struct node* r)
{
   if(r!=NULL){
      printf("%d ", r->value);
      preOrder(r->left);
      preOrder(r->right);
   }
}
void postOrder(struct node* r)
{
   if(r!=NULL){
      postOrder(r->left);
      postOrder(r->right);
      printf("%d ", r->value);
   }
}
```

## 4.11.  Priority Queues (Heaps)

Queues are a standard mechanism for ordering tasks on a first-come, first-served basis

Priority queues

- Store tasks using a partial ordering based on priority
- Ensure highest priority task at head of queue

Heaps are the underlying data structure of priority queues

Main operations

1.  Insert (i.e., enqueue)

- Dynamic insert
- specification of a priority level (0-high, 1,2.. Low)

2. DeleteMin (i.e., dequeue)

- Finds the current minimum element (read: "highest priority") in the queue, deletes it from the queue, and returns it

## 4.12. Binary Heap

A binary heap is a binary tree with two properties

1. Structure property
2. Heap order Property

### 1. *Structure Property: A Binary Heap is a Complete Binary Tree*

- Each level (except possibly the bottom most level) is completely filled
- The bottom most level may be partially filled (from left to right)

It is a complete binary tree of height 'h' has between $2^h$ and $2^{h+1}-1$ nodes. As it represented as array it doesn't require pointers and also the operations requires to traverse the tree are extremely simple and fast. The only disadvantage is to specify the maximum heap size in the advance.

Its height =0 (log N).

### 2. *Heap Order Property (Min Heap)*

1. Heap-order property (for a "MinHeap")
- For every node X, key(parent(X)) ≤ key(X)
- Except root node, which has no parent
2. Thus minimum key always at root
- Alternatively, for a "MaxHeap", always keep the maximum key at the root

   Insert and deleteMin must maintain heap order property

   The ordering can be one of two types:

- the *min-heap property*: the value of each node is greater than or equal to the value of its parent, with the minimum-value element at the root.
- the *max-heap property*: the value of each node is less than or equal to the value of its parent, with the maximum-value element at the root.

Example for min heap and max heap

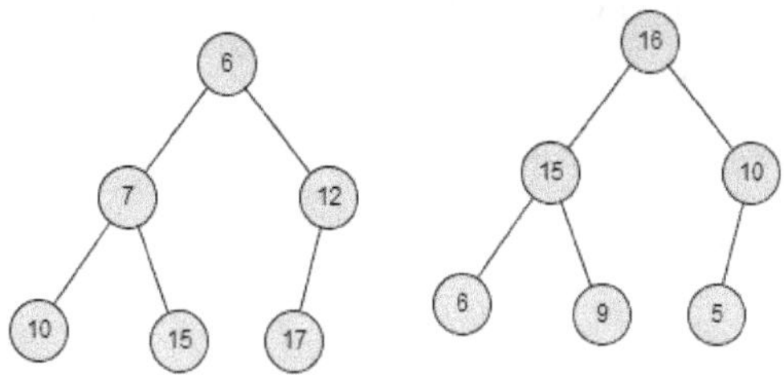

In a heap the highest (or lowest) priority element is always stored at the root, hence the name "heap". A heap is not a sorted structure and can be regarded as partially ordered. As you see from the picture, there is no particular relationship among nodes on any given level, even among the siblings.

Since a heap is a complete binary tree, it has a smallest possible height - a heap with N nodes always has O(log N) height. A heap is useful data structure when you need to remove the object with the highest (or lowest) priority. A common use of a heap is to implement a priority queue.

### *Array Implementation*

A complete binary tree can be uniquely represented by storing its level order traversal in an array.

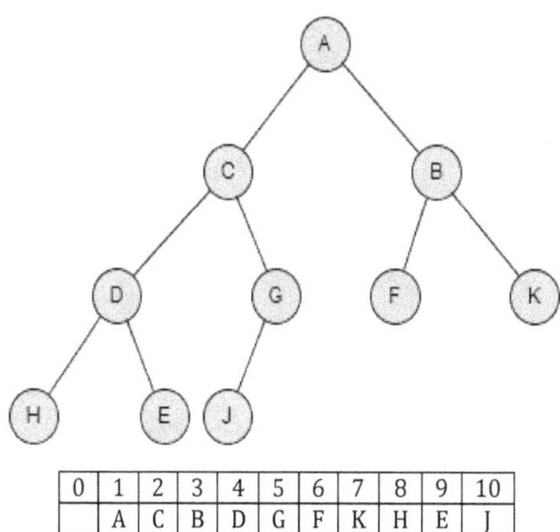

| 0 | 1 | 2 | 3 | 4 | 5 | 6 | 7 | 8 | 9 | 10 |
|---|---|---|---|---|---|---|---|---|---|----|
|   | A | C | B | D | G | F | K | H | E | J  |

The root is the second item in the array. We skip the index zero cell of the array for the convenience of implementation.

Consider k-th element of the array, the

its left child is located at 2*k index

its right child is located at 2*k+1. index

its parent is located at k/2 index

### Insert

The new element is initially appended to the end of the heap (as the last element of the array). The heap property is repaired by comparing the added element with its parent and moving the added element up a level (swapping positions with the parent). This process is called "percolation up". The comparison is repeated until the parent is larger than or equal to the percolating element.

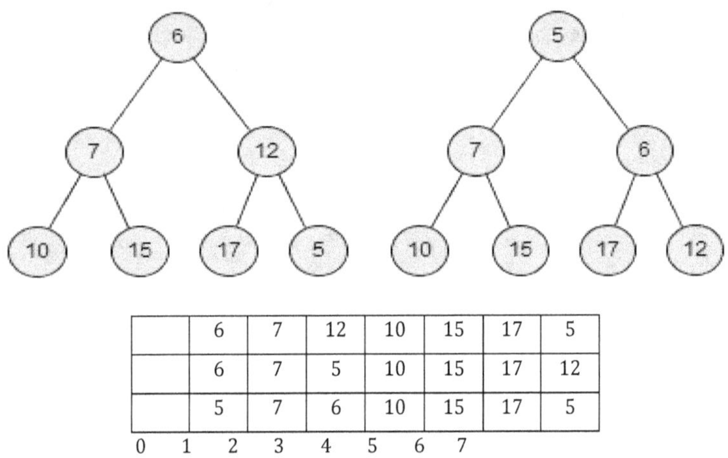

| | 6 | 7 | 12 | 10 | 15 | 17 | 5 |
|---|---|---|---|---|---|---|---|
| | 6 | 7 | 5 | 10 | 15 | 17 | 12 |
| | 5 | 7 | 6 | 10 | 15 | 17 | 5 |

0   1   2   3   4   5   6   7

### Delete Min

The minimum element can be found at the root, which is the first element of the array.

We remove the root and replace it with the last element of the heap and then restore the heap property by percolating down. Similar to insertion, the worst-case runtime is O{log n).

### Binary Heap

The algorithm runs in two steps. Given an array of data, first, we build a heap and then turn it into a sorted list by calling deleteMin. The running time of the algorithm is O(n log n).

Example 1: Given an array **A= {5,10,15,7,3}** We will sort it with the Heap Sort (Min Heap).

Insert element as structure property 5 as root, 10 as left child, 15 as right child

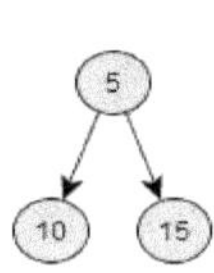

Insert 7 check for min heap condition

Swap 10 with 7

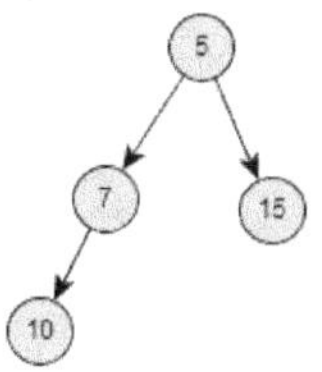

Insert 3 and check for heap condition

Swap last element 3 with 7 ,3 with 5 (Min Heap)

**Delete Min:**

Replace first element 3 by last element 7 and remove 3

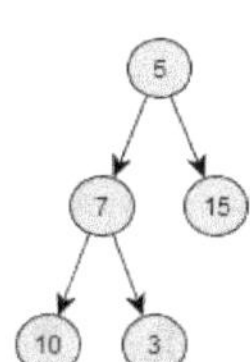

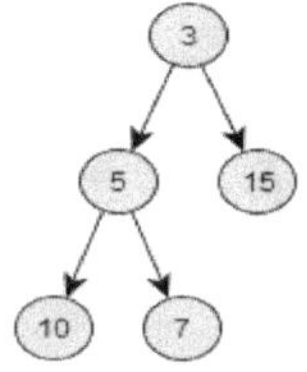

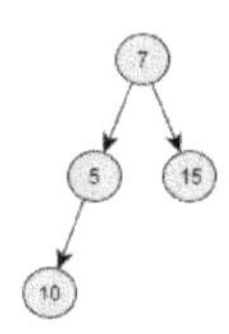

Swap 5 with 7(Heap)

Replace first element 5 by last element 10 and remove 5

Swap 10 with 7(Heap)

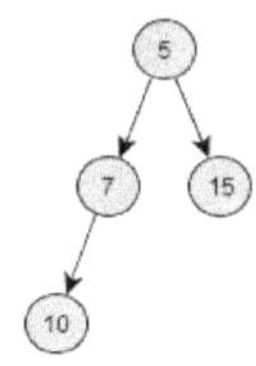

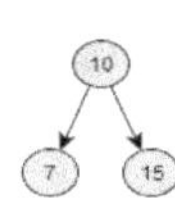

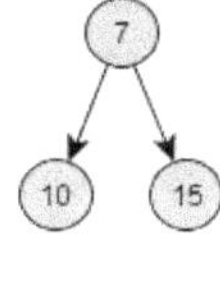

Replace first element 7 by last element 15 and remove 7

Swap 10 with 15(Heap)

Replace first element 10 by last element 15 and remove 10

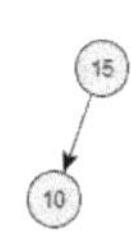

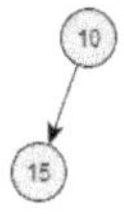

The sorted array after deletemin is

| 3 | 5 | 7 | 10 | 15 |
|---|---|---|----|----|

Example 2: Given an array B= {25, 30, 15, 17, 8, 11, 16, 33, 44, 40} We will sort it with the Heap Sort.

Inert 25

Insert 30 as left child

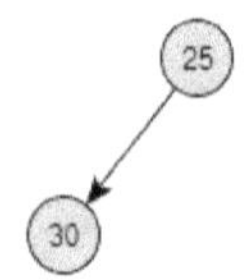

Insert 15 as right child

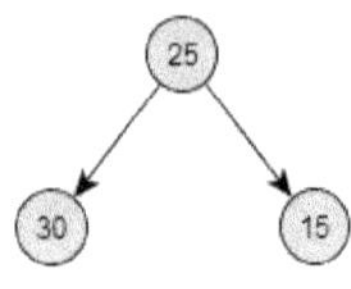

As root has greater value 25 swap with the min value node 15.

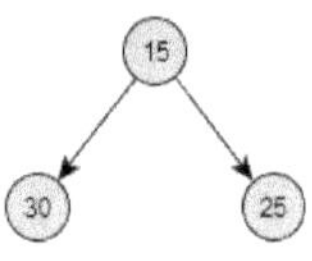

Insert 17

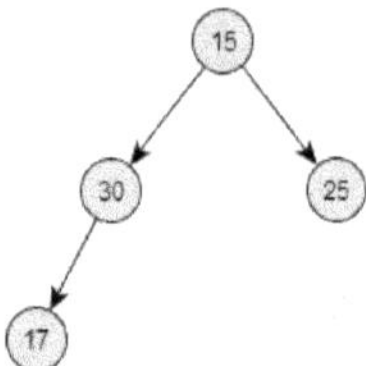

Swap 30 with 17 to satisfy heap property

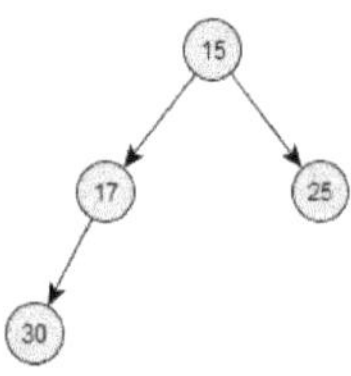

Insert 8

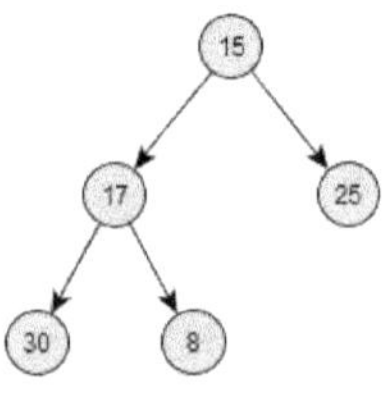

Swap 8 with 17 to satisfy heap property

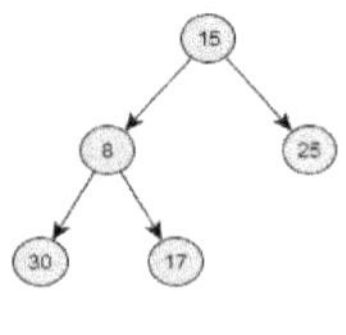

Swap 8 with 15 to satisfy heap property

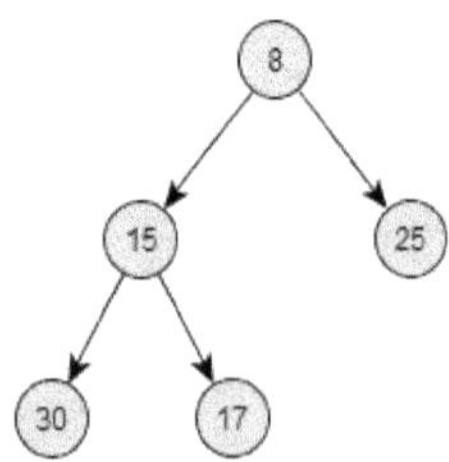

Insert 11

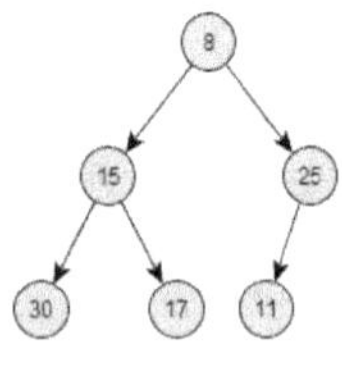

## Swap 11 with 25

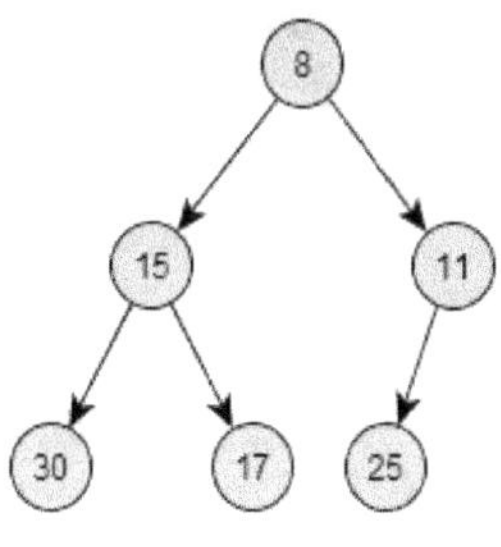

## Insert 16

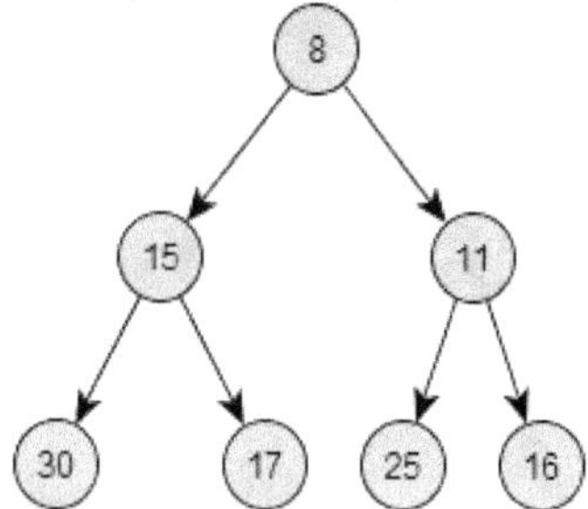

## Insert 33

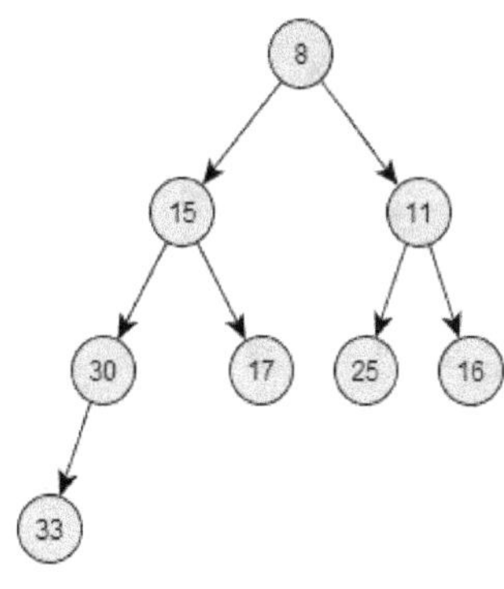

## Insert 44

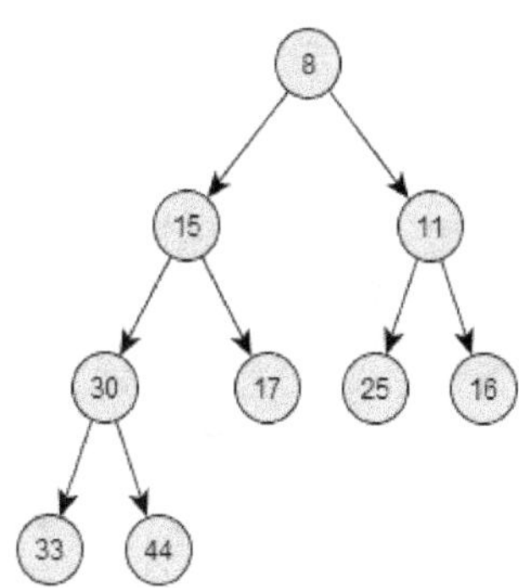

## Insert 40

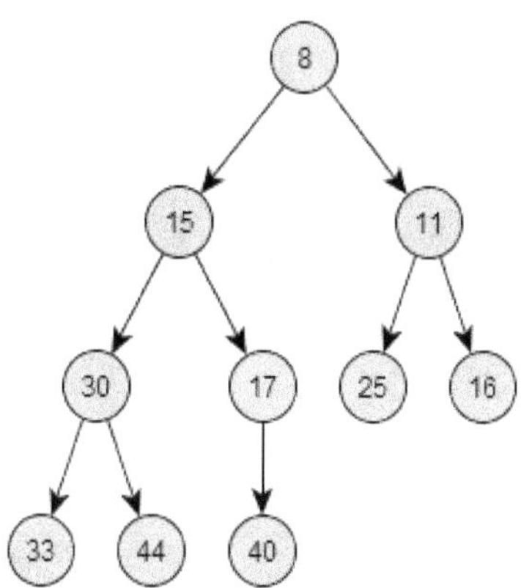

Delete Min operation:

Delete 8(Replace with the last element 40)

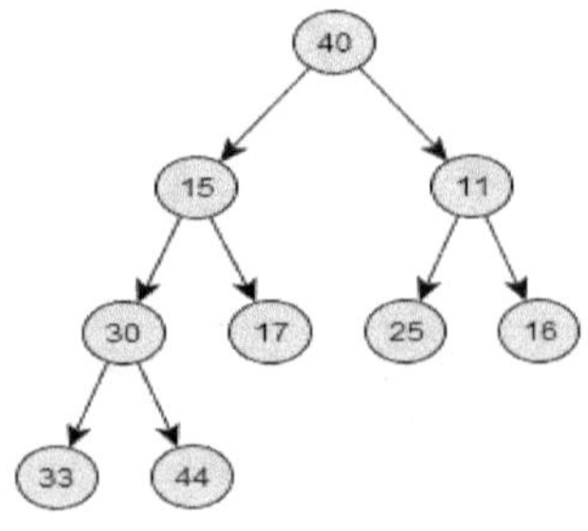

Check for heap condition. swap 40 with 11 and 11 with 16

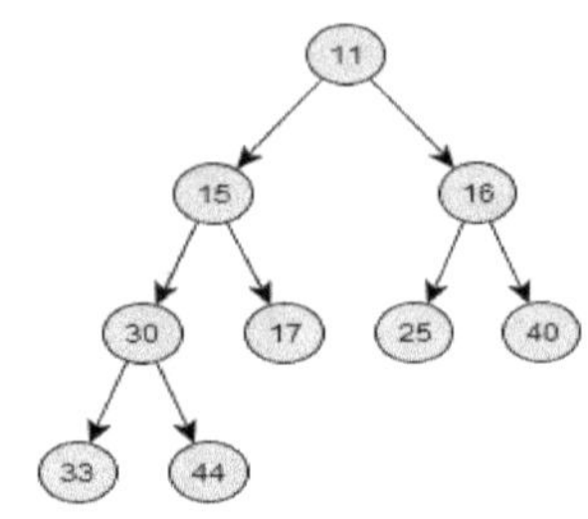

Delete 11(Replace with the last element 44)

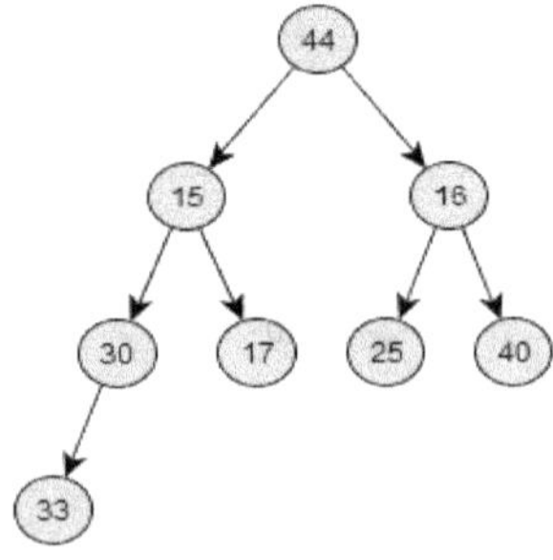

Swap 44 with 15

Swap 44 with 17

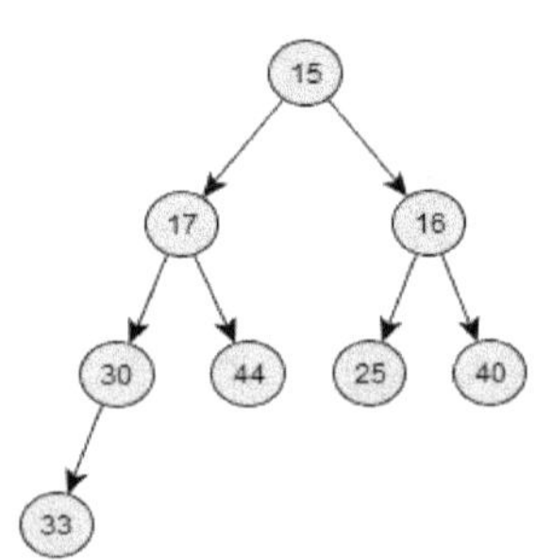

Delete 15(Replace with the last element 33)

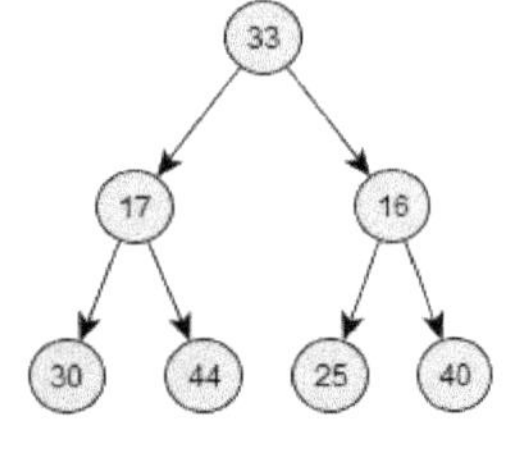

Swap 16 with 33

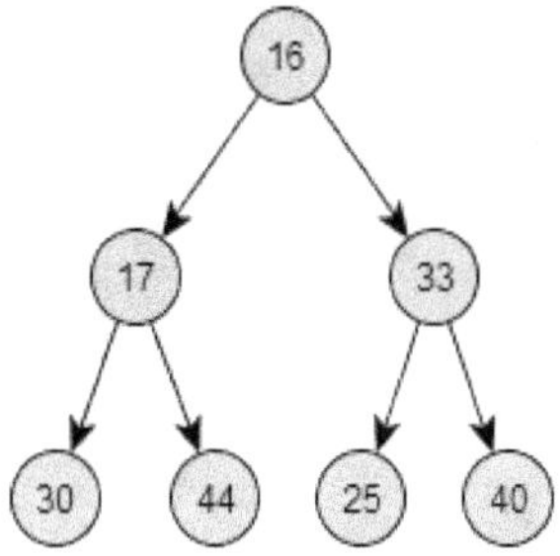

Swap 25 with 33

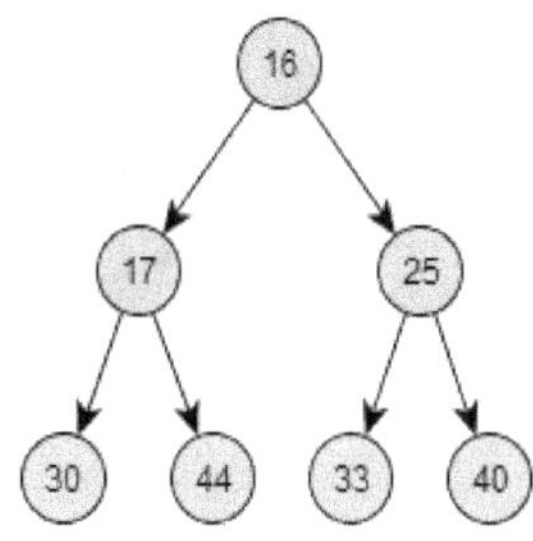

Delete 16(Replace with the last element 40)

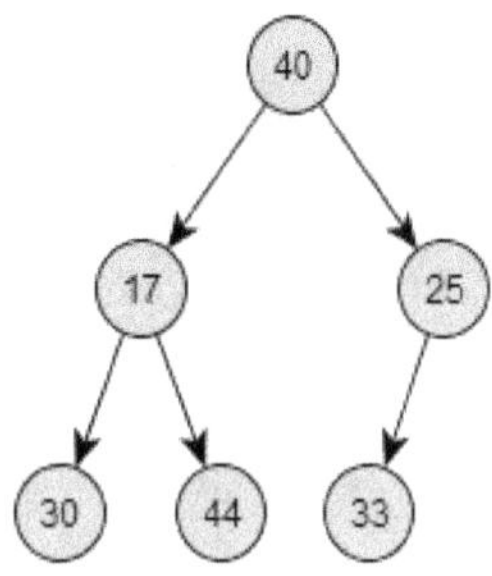

Swap 17 with 40

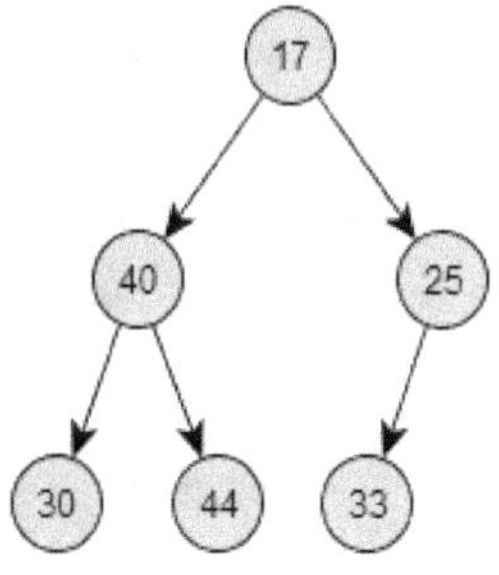

Delete 17(Replace with the last element 33)

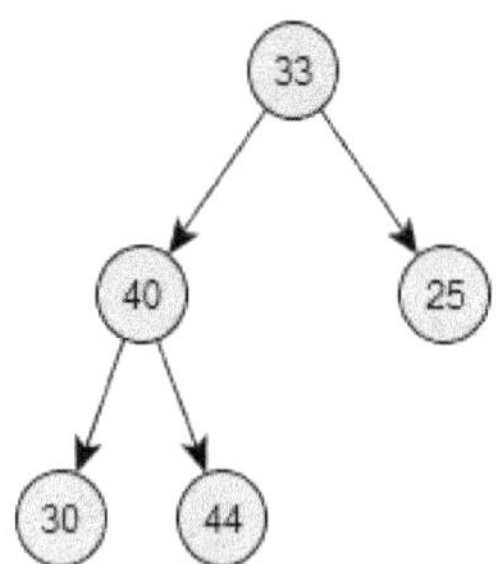

Swap 25 with 33

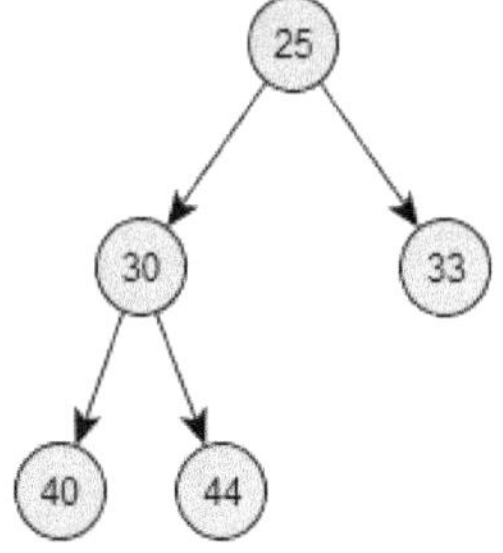

Delete 25(Replace with the last element 44)    Swap 44 with 30 and 40 with 44

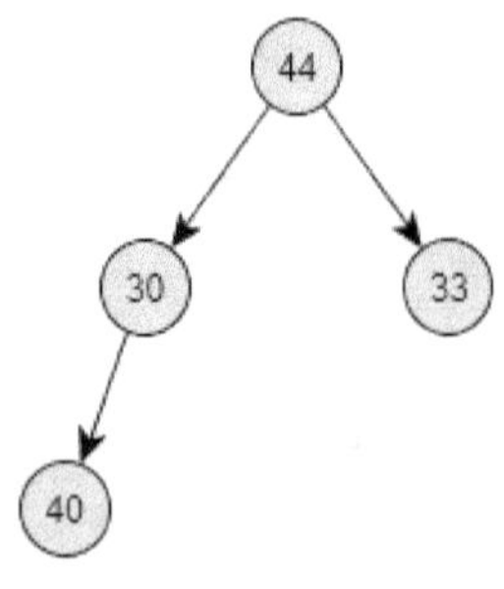

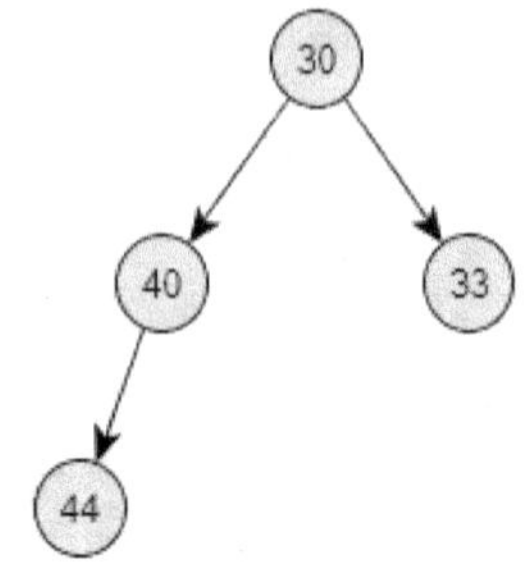

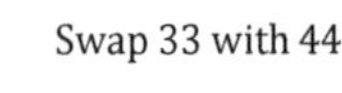

Delete 30(Replace with the last element 44)           Swap 33 with 44

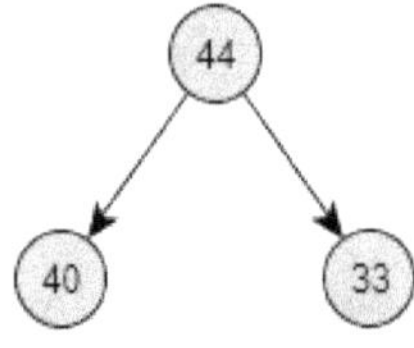

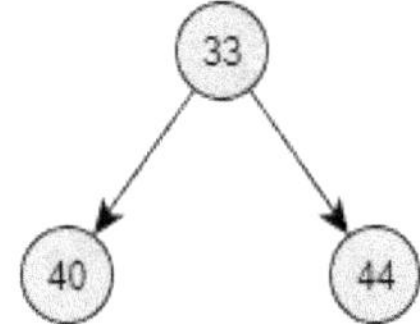

Delete 33(Replace with the last element 44)           Swap 40 with 44

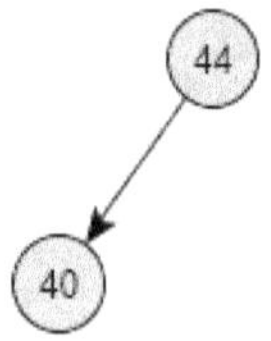

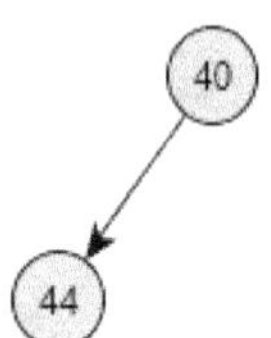

Delete 40(Replace with the last element 44)

The sorted array after deletemin is

| 8 | 11 | 15 | 16 | 17 | 25 | 30 | 33 | 40 | 44 |
|---|----|----|----|----|----|----|----|----|----|

### *Program for Binary Heap*

```c
#include<stdio.h>
#include<conio.h>
int temp,ap;
void input(int *a,int n)
{
   int i;
   printf("Enter %d elements....\n",n);
   for(i=0;i<n;i++)
     scanf("%d",&a[i]);
}
void output(int *a,int n)
{
   int i;
   for(i=0;i<n;i++)
     printf("%d,",a[i]);
}void maxheap(int *a,int i,int n)
{
   int child,temp;
   for(temp=a[i];(2*i+1)<n;i=child)
   {
     child= 2*i+1;
     if((child!=n-1)&&(a[child+1]>a[child]))
       child++;
     if(temp<a[child])
       a[i]=a[child];
     else
       break;
   }
   a[i]=temp;
}
void heapsort(int *a,int n)
```

```c
{
    int i;
    for(i=n/2;i>=0;i--)
    {
        maxheap(a,i,n);
    }
    for(i=n-1;i>=0;i--)
    {
        int t;
        t=a[0];
        a[0]=a[i];
        a[i]=t;
        maxheap(a,0,i);
    }
}
int main()
{
    int a[25],n;
        printf("Enter the no of elements...");
        scanf("%d",&n);
        input(a,n);
        printf("\nThe elements in the array before sorting...");
        output(a,n);
        heapsort(a,n);
        printf("\nThe elements in the array after sorting...");
        output(a,n);
}
```

━━━━━━━━━━━━ **CHAPTER 5** ━━━━━━━━━━━━

# BALANCED TREES

## 5.1.  AVL Trees

AVL tree is a self-balanced binary search tree. That means, an AVL tree is also a binary search tree but it is a balanced tree. A binary tree is said to be balanced, if the difference between the heights of left and right subtrees of every node in the tree is either -1, 0 or +1.

In other words, a binary tree is said to be balanced if for every node, height of its children differs by at most one. In an AVL tree, every node maintains a extra information known as balance factor. The AVL tree was introduced in the year of 1962 by G.M. Adelson-Velsky and E.M. Landis. An AVL tree is a balanced binary search tree. In an AVL tree, balance factor of every node is either -1, 0 or +1.

Balance factor of a node is the difference between the heights of left and right subtrees of that node. The balance factor of a node is calculated either height of left subtree-height of right subtree (OR) height of right subtree-height of left subtree. In the following explanation, we are calculating as follows.

**Balance factor = height of Left Subtree – height of Right Subtree**

Example:

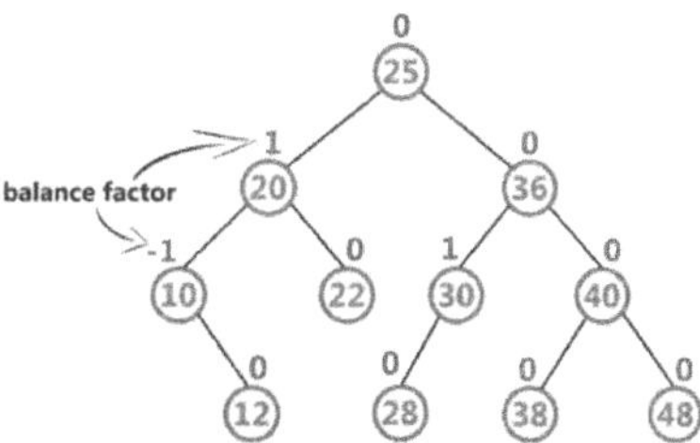


The above tree is a binary search tree and every node is satisfying balance factor condition. So this tree is said to be an AVL tree. Every AVL Tree is a binary search tree but all the Binary Search Trees need not to be AVL trees.

### *AVL Tree Rotations*

AVL tree, after performing every operation like insertion and deletion we need to check the balance factor of every node in the tree. If every node satisfies the balance factor condition, then we conclude the operation otherwise we must make it balanced. We use rotation operations to make the tree balanced whenever the tree is becoming imbalanced due to any operation.

Rotation operations are used to make a tree balanced. Rotation is the process of moving the nodes to either left or right to make tree balanced. There are four rotations and they are classified into two types.

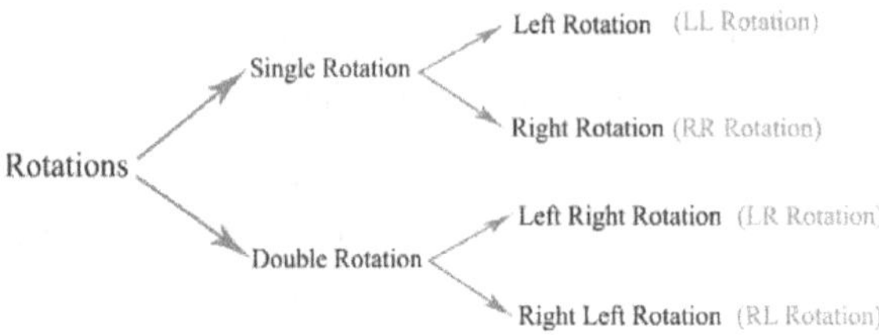


## Single Left Rotation (LL Rotation)

In LL Rotation, every node moves one position to left from the current position. To understand LL Rotation, let us consider following insertion operations into an AVL Tree.

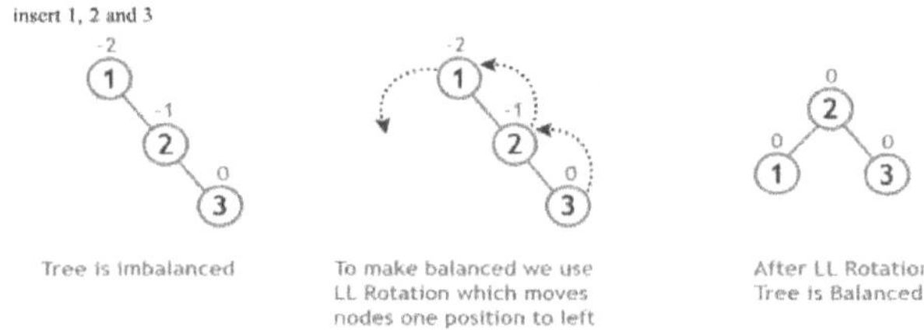


## Single Right Rotation (RR Rotation)

In RR Rotation, every node moves one position to right from the current position. To understand RR Rotation, let us consider following insertion operations into an AVL Tree.

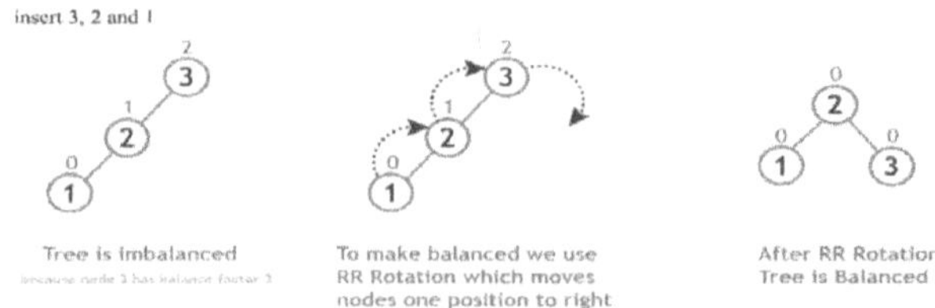

### *Left Right Rotation (LR Rotation)*

The LR Rotation is combination of single left rotation followed by single right rotation. In LR Rotation, first every node moves one position to left then one position to right from the current position. To understand LR Rotation, let us consider following insertion operations into an AVL Tree.

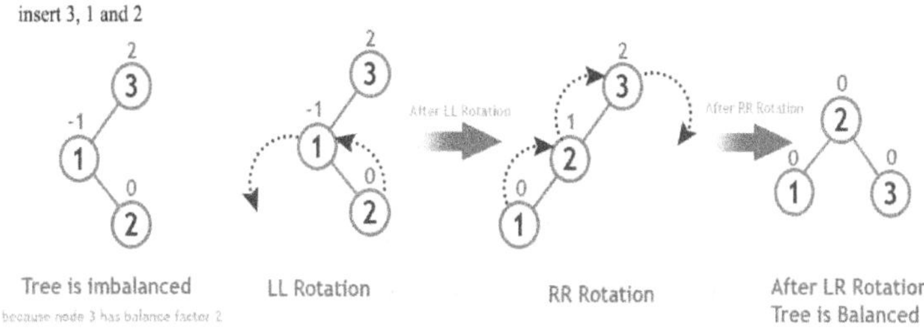



### *Right Left Rotation (RL Rotation)*

The RL Rotation is combination of single right rotation followed by single left rotation. In RL Rotation, first every node moves one position to right then one position to left from the current position. To understand RL Rotation, let us consider following insertion operations into an AVL Tree.

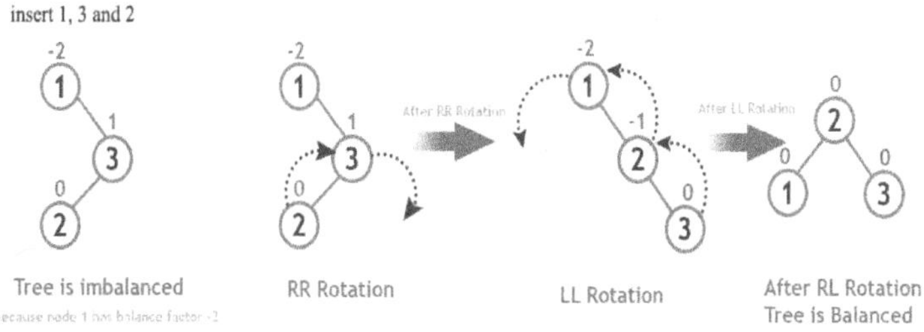



### *Operations in an AVL Tree*

The following operations are performed on an AVL tree.

- Search

- Insertion
- Deletion

## 1. Search Operation in AVL Tree

In an AVL tree, the search operation is performed with O(log n) time complexity.

The search operation is performed similar to Binary search tree search operation.

### Algorithm

**Step 1:** Read the search element from the user

**Step 2:** Compare, the search element with the value of root node in the tree.

**Step 3:** If both are matching, then display "Given node found!!!" and terminate the function

**Step 4:** If both are not matching, then check whether search element is smaller or larger than that node value.

**Step 5:** If search element is smaller, then continue the search process in left subtree.

**Step 6:** If search element is larger, then continue the search process in right subtree.

**Step 7:** Repeat the same until we found exact element or we completed with a leaf node

**Step 8:** If we reach to the node with search value, then display "Element is found" and terminate the function.

**Step 9:** If we reach to a leaf node and it is also not matching, then display "Element not found" and terminate the function.

## 2. Insertion Operation in AVL Tree

In an AVL tree, the insertion operation is performed with O(log n) time complexity.

In AVL Tree, new node is always inserted as a leaf node.

### Algorithm

**Step 1:** Insert the new element into the tree using Binary Search Tree insertion logic.

**Step 2:** After insertion, check the Balance Factor of every node.

**Step 3:** If the Balance Factor of every node is 0 or 1 or -1 then go for next operation.

**Step 4:** If the Balance Factor of any node is other than 0 or 1 or -1 then tree is said to be imbalanced. Then perform the suitable Rotation to make it balanced. And go for next operation.

### Routine

```
tree insert(int x,tree t)
{
if(t==NULL)
{
t->data=x;
t->left=t->right=NULL;
t->ht=0;
}
else if (x<t->data)
{
t->left=insert(x,t->left);
if(BF(t)==2)
if(x<t->left->data)
t=LL(t);
else
t=LR(t);
}
else if (x>t->data)
{
t->right=insert(x,t->right);
if(BF(t)==-2)
if(x>t->right->data)
t=RR(t);
else
t=RL(t);
}
t->ht=height(t);
return(t);
}
```

## Example: Construct an AVL Tree by inserting numbers from 1 to 8.

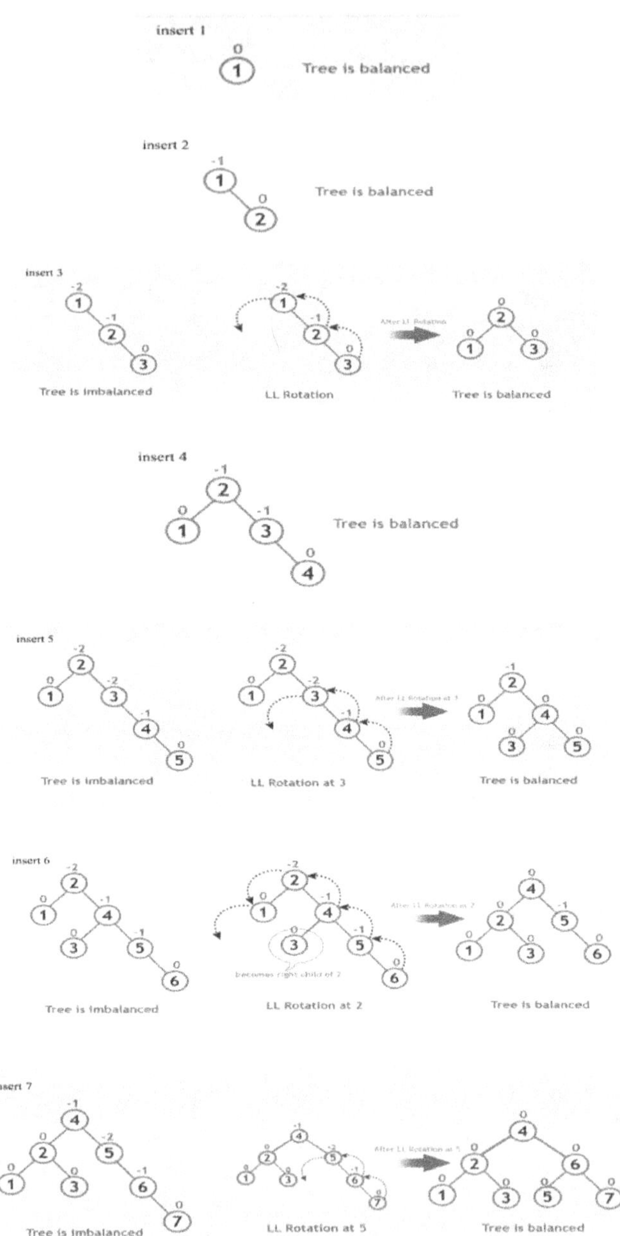

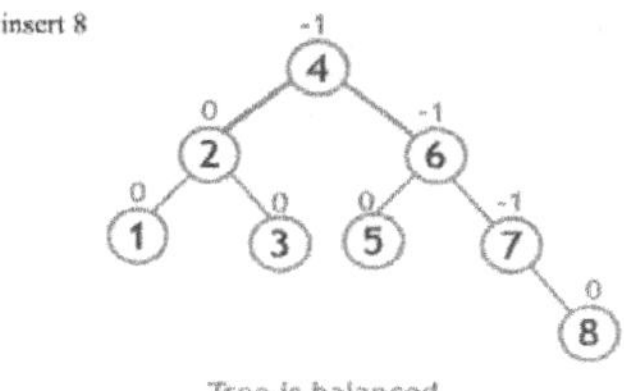


## 3. Deletion Operation in AVL Tree

In an AVL Tree, the deletion operation is similar to deletion operation in BST. But after every deletion operation we need to check with the Balance Factor condition. If the tree is balanced after deletion, then go for next operation otherwise perform the suitable rotation to make the tree Balanced.

## Program for AVL Trees

```c
#include<stdio.h>
#include<conio.h>
struct avltree
{
int data;
int ht;
struct avltree *left;
struct avltree *right;
};
typedef struct avltree *tree;
tree t,x,y;
tree insert(int x,tree t);
void preorder(tree t);
int height(tree t);
int BF(tree t);
tree *rotateright(tree x);
tree *rotateleft(tree x);
tree *RR(tree t);
tree *LL(tree t);
tree *LR(tree t);
```

```c
tree *RL(tree t);
tree insert(int x,tree t)
{
if(t==NULL)
{
t->data=x;
t->left=t->right=NULL;
t->ht=0;
}
else if (x<t->data)
{
t->left=insert(x,t->left);
if(BF(t)==2)
if(x<t->left->data)
t=LL(t);
else
t=LR(t);
}
else if (x>t->data)
{
t->right=insert(x,t->right);
if(BF(t)==-2)
if(x>t->right->data)
t=RR(t);
else
t=RL(t);
}
t->ht=height(t);
return(t);
}
tree *RR(tree t)
{
t=rotateleft(t);
```

```
return(t);
}
tree *LL(tree t)
{
t=rotateright(t);
return(t);
}
tree *RL(tree t)
{
t->right=rotateright(t->right);
t=rotateleft(t);
return(t);
}
tree *LR(tree t)
{
t->left=rotateleft(t->left);
t=rotateright(t);
return(t);
}
int BF(tree t)
{
int lh,rh;
if(t==NULL)
return (0);
if(t->left==NULL)
lh=0;
else
lh=1+t->left->ht;
if(t->right==NULL)
rh=0;
else
rh=1+t->right->ht;
return(lh-rh);
```

```c
}
int height(tree t)
{
int lh,rh;
if(t==NULL)
return (0);
if(t->left==NULL)
lh=0;
else
lh=1+t->left->ht;
if(t->right==NULL)
rh=0;
else
rh=1+t->right->ht;
if(lh>rh)
return(lh);
return(rh);
}
void preorder(tree t)
{
if(t!=NULL)
{
printf("%d",t->data);
preorder(t->left);
preorder(t->right);
}}
void main()
{
int n,i,x,op;
tree t=NULL;
clrscr();
do
{
```

```c
printf("1.insert 2.display");
scanf("%d",&op);
switch(op)
{
case 1:
printf("enter element");
scanf("%d",&x);
t=insert(x,t);
break;
case 2:
preorder(t);
break;
}}while(op!=3);
}
tree *rotateright(tree x)
{
tree y;
y=x->left;
x->left=y->right;
y->right=x;
x->ht=height(x);
y->ht=height(y);
return(y);
}
tree *rotateleft(tree x)
{
tree y;
y=x->right;
x->right=y->left;
y->left=x;
x->ht=height(x);
y->ht=height(y);
return(y); }
```

## *Example*

37,14,23,20,13,27,19,44,57,50,7

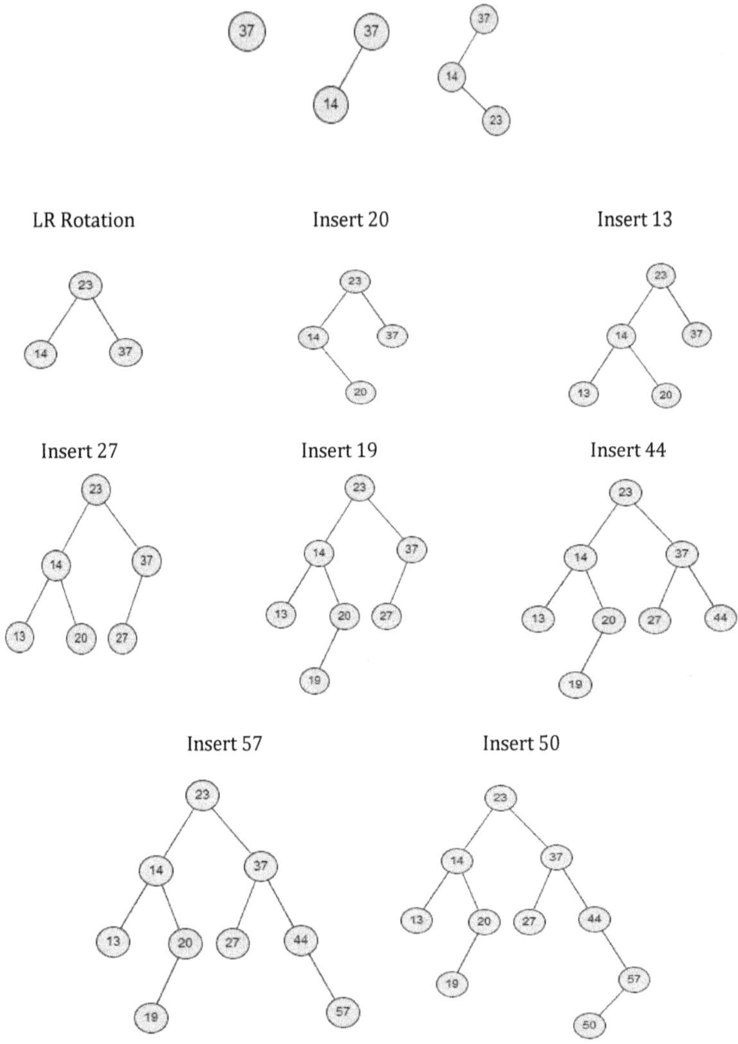

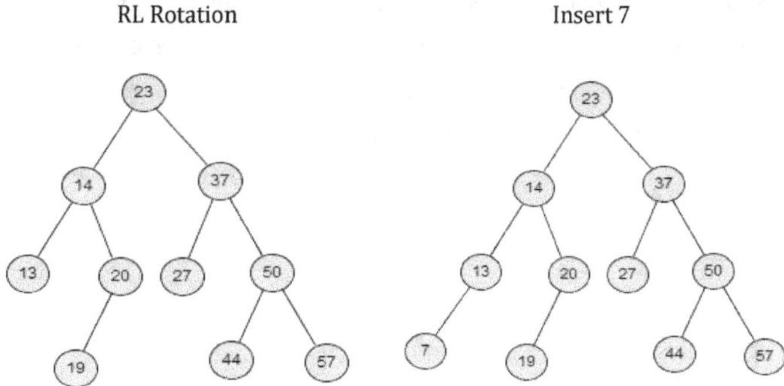



## 5.2.   Splay Trees

A splay tree is a self-adjusting binary search tree with the additional property that recently accessed elements are quick to access again. It performs basic operations such as insertion, look-up and removal in O(log n) amortized time. A good example is a network router.

### *Search Operation*

The search operation in Splay tree does the standard BST search, in addition to search, it also splays (move a node to the root). If the search is successful, then the node that is found is splayed and becomes the new root. Else the last node accessed prior to reaching the NULL is splayed and becomes the new root. There are following cases for the node being accessed.

1. **Node is root** We simply return the root, don't do anything else as the accessed node is already root.

2. **Zig: Node is child of root**(the node has no grandparent). Node is either a left child of root (we do a right rotation) or node is a right child of its parent (we do a left rotation). T1, T2 and T3 are subtrees of the tree rooted with y (on left side) or x (on right side)

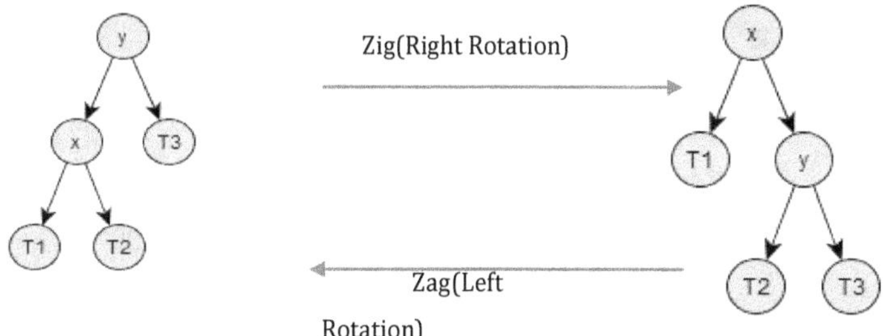

3. **Node has both parent and grandparent** There can be following subcases.

   **a) Zig-Zig and Zag-Zag** Node is left child of parent and parent is also left child of grandparent (Two right rotations) or node is right child of its parent and parent is also right child of grandparent (Two Left Rotations).

## *Zig-Zig (Left Left Case)*

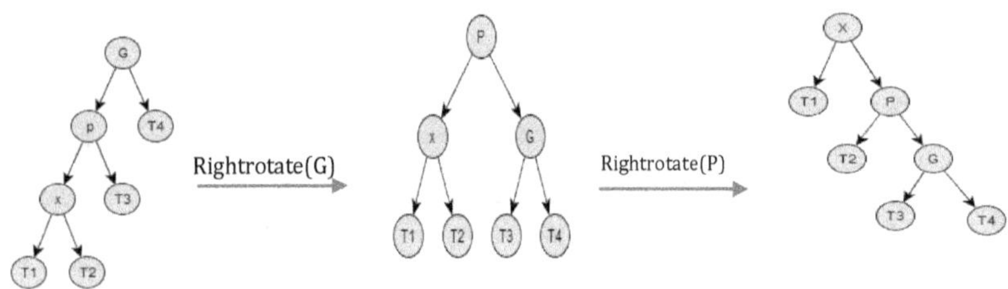

## *Zag-zag(Right Right case)*

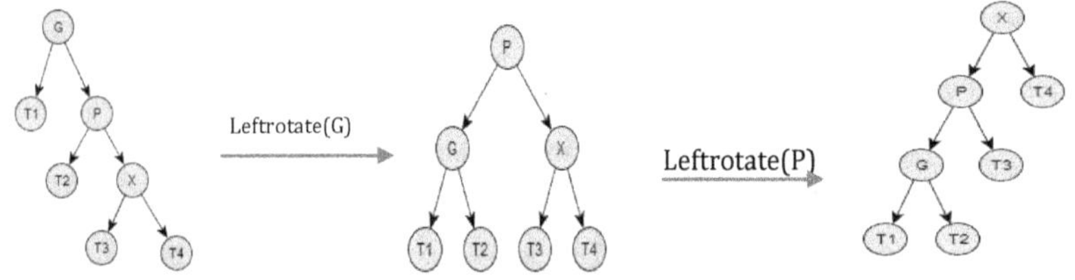

   **b) Zig-Zag and Zag-Zig** Node is left child of parent and parent is right child of grand parent (Left Rotation followed by right rotation) or node is right child of its parent and parent is left child of grand parent (Right Rotation followed by left rotation).

## *Zig-Zag(Left Right case)*

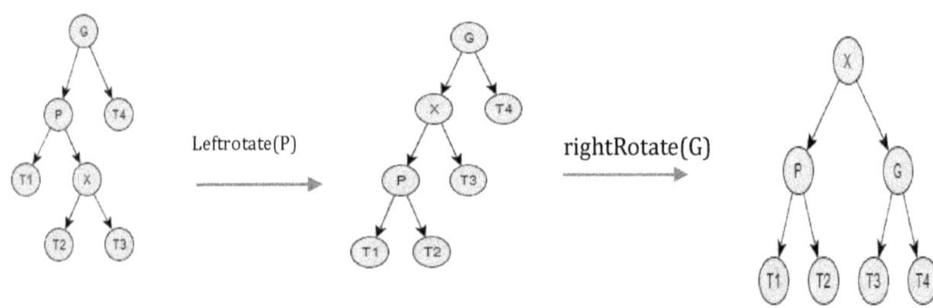

### *Zag-Zig(Right Left case)*

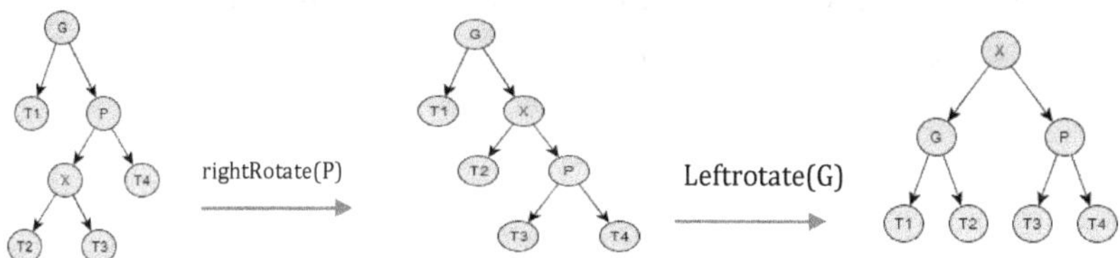


### *Example*

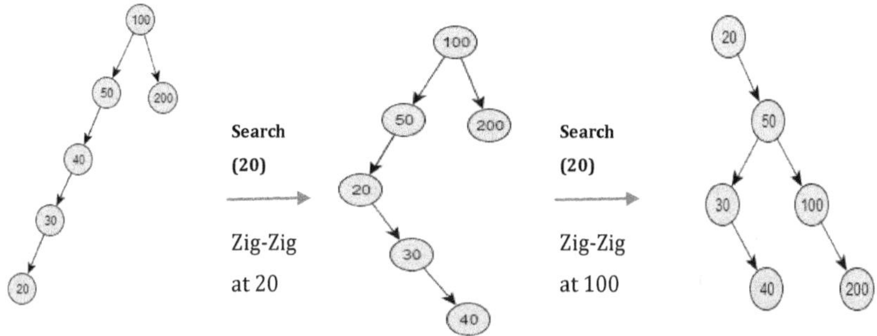


The important thing to note is, the search or splay operation not only brings the searched key to root, but also balances the BST. For example, in above case, height of BST is reduced by 1.

### *Insertion*

Splay tree is a self-balancing data structure where the last accessed key is always at root. The insert operation is similar to Binary Search Tree insert with additional steps to make sure that the newly inserted key becomes the new root.

Following are different cases to insert a key k in splay tree.

1. Root is NULL: We simply allocate a new node and return it as root.
2. Splay the given key k. If k is already present, then it becomes the new root. If not present, then last accessed leaf node becomes the new root.
3. If new root's key is same as k, don't do anything as k is already present.
4. Else allocate memory for new node and compare root's key with k.

   **a)** If k is smaller than root's key, make root as right child of new node, copy left child of root as left child of new node and make left child of root as NULL.

**b)** If k is greater than root's key, make root as left child of new node, copy right child of root as right child of new node and make right child of root as NULL.

5. Return new node as new root of tree.

## Example

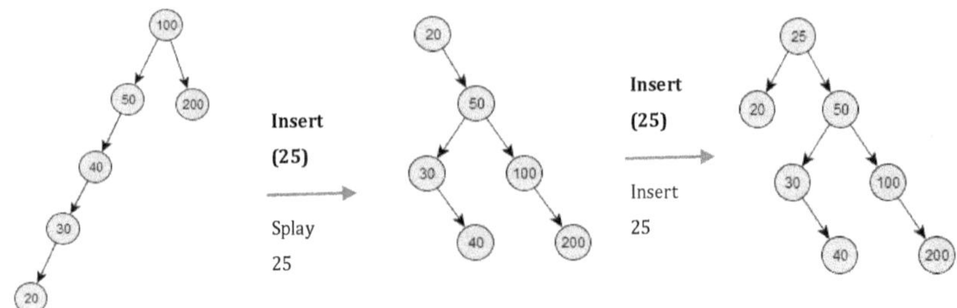


## Program for Splay Tree

```c
#include<stdio.h>
#include<stdlib.h>
struct node
{
  int key;
  struct node *left, *right;
};
struct node* newNode(int key)
{
  struct node* node = (struct node*)malloc(sizeof(struct node));
  node->key  = key;
  node->left = node->right = NULL;
  return (node);
}
struct node *rightRotate(struct node *x)
{
  struct node *y = x->left;
  x->left = y->right;
  y->right = x;
  return y;
}
```

```c
struct node *leftRotate(struct node *x)
{
    struct node *y = x->right;
    x->right = y->left;
    y->left = x;
    return y;
}
struct node *splay(struct node *root, int key)
{
    // Base cases: root is NULL or key is present at root
    if (root == NULL || root->key == key)
        return root;
    // Key lies in left subtree
    if (root->key > key)
    {
        // Key is not in tree, we are done
        if (root->left == NULL) return root;
        // Zig-Zig (Left Left)
        if (root->left->key > key)
        {
            // First recursively bring the key as root of left-left
            root->left->left = splay(root->left->left, key);
            // Do first rotation for root, second rotation is done after else
            root = rightRotate(root);
        }
        else if (root->left->key < key) // Zig-Zag (Left Right)
        {
            // First recursively bring the key as root of left-right
            root->left->right = splay(root->left->right, key);
            // Do first rotation for root->left
            if (root->left->right != NULL)
                root->left = leftRotate(root->left);
        }
        // Do second rotation for root
```

```c
        return (root->left == NULL)? root: rightRotate(root);
    }
    else // Key lies in right subtree
    {
        // Key is not in tree, we are done
        if (root->right == NULL) return root;
        // Zag-Zig (Right Left)
        if (root->right->key > key)
        {
            // Bring the key as root of right-left
            root->right->left = splay(root->right->left, key);
            // Do first rotation for root->right
            if (root->right->left != NULL)
                root->right = rightRotate(root->right);
        }
        else if (root->right->key < key)// Zag-Zag (Right Right)
        {
            // Bring the key as root of right-right and do first rotation
            root->right->right = splay(root->right->right, key);
            root = leftRotate(root);
        }
        // Do second rotation for root
        return (root->right == NULL)? root: leftRotate(root);
    }
}
struct node *search(struct node *root, int key)
{
    return splay(root, key);
}
void preOrder(struct node *root)
{
    if (root != NULL)
    {
        printf("%d ", root->key);
```

```
      preOrder(root->left);
      preOrder(root->right);
   }
}
 int main()
{
    struct node *root = newNode(100);
    root->left = newNode(50);
    root->right = newNode(200);
    root->left->left = newNode(40);
    root->left->left->left = newNode(30);
    root->left->left->left->left = newNode(20);
    root = search(root, 20);
    printf("Preorder traversal of the modified Splay tree is \n");
    preOrder(root);
    return 0;
}
```

## 5.3.  B-Trees

In a binary search tree, AVL Tree, Red-Black tree etc., every node can have only one value (key) and maximum of two children but there is another type of search tree called B-Tree in which a node can store more than one value (key) and it can have more than two children. B-Tree was developed in the year of 1972 by Bayer and McCreight with the name Height Balanced m-way Search Tree. Later it was named as B-Tree. B-Tree can be defined as follows.

B-Tree is a self-balanced search tree with multiple keys in every node and more than two children for every node. Here, number of keys in a node and number of children for a node is depend on the order of the B-Tree. Every B-Tree has order.

B-Tree of Order m has the following properties.

**Property 1** - All the leaf nodes must be at same level.

**Property 2** - All nodes except root must have at least [m/2]-1 keys and maximum of m-1 keys.

**Property 3** - All non leaf nodes except root (i.e. all internal nodes) must have at least m/2 children.

**Property 4** - If the root node is a non leaf node, then it must have at least 2 children.

**Property 5** - A non leaf node with n-1 keys must have n number of children.

**Property 6** - All the key values within a node must be in Ascending Order.

For example, B-Tree of Order 4 contains maximum 3 key values in a node and maximum 4 children for a node.

## *Example*

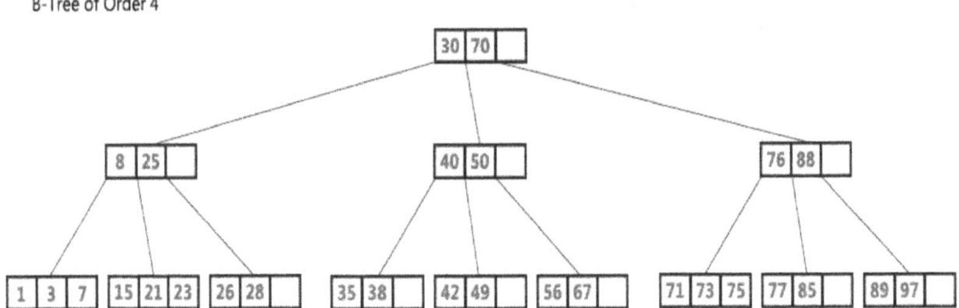


## *Operations in a B-Tree*

The following operations are performed on a B-Tree.

- Search
- Insertion
- Deletion

## *1. Search Operation in B-Tree*

In a B-Tree, the search operation is similar to that of Binary Search Tree. In a Binary search tree, the search process starts from the root node and every time we make a 2-way decision (we go to either left subtree or right subtree). In B-Tree also search process starts from the root node but every time we make n-way decision where n is the total number of children that node has. In a B-Tree, the search operation is performed with O(log n) time complexity

## *Algorithm*

**Step 1:** Read the search element from the user

**Step 2:** Compare, the search element with first key value of root node in the tree.

**Step 3:** If both are matching, then display "Given node found!!!" and terminate the function

**Step 4:** If both are not matching, then check whether search element is smaller or larger than that key value.

**Step 5:** If search element is smaller, then continue the search process in left subtree.

**Step 6:** If search element is larger, then compare with next key value in the same node and repeat step 3, 4, 5 and 6 until we found exact match or comparison completed with last key value in a leaf node.

**Step 7:** If we completed with last key value in a leaf node, then display "Element is not found" and terminate the function.

### 2.  *Insertion Operation in B-Tree*

In a B-Tree, the new element must be added only at leaf node. That means, always the new key Value is attached to leaf node only.

### *Algorithm*

**Step 1:** Check whether tree is Empty.

**Step 2:** If tree is Empty, then create a new node with new key value and insert into the tree as a root node.

**Step 3:** If tree is Not Empty, then find a leaf node to which the new key value cab be added using Binary Search Tree logic.

**Step 4:** If that leaf node has an empty position, then add the new key value to that leaf node by maintaining ascending order of key value within the node.

**Step 5:** If that leaf node is already full, then split that leaf node by sending middle value to its parent node. Repeat the same until sending value is fixed into a node.

**Step 6:** If the splitting is occurring to the root node, then the middle value becomes new root node for the tree and the height of the tree is increased by one.

### *Example*

Construct a **B-Tree of Order 3** by inserting numbers from 1 to 10.

### *Insert 1*

1 is the first element to be inserted so it acts as root node.

### Insert 2

2 is added to existing leaf node. The leaf has empty position. So,new element is added to that empty position.

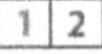

### Insert 3

3 is added to the existing leaf node. But that has no empty position. So, we split that node by inserting the middle value 2 to its parent node. Now, the middle value becomes the root node.

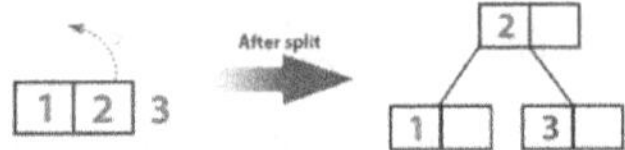

### Insert 4

Element 4 is larger than root node. So, move to right of 2. We reach a leaf node with value 3 and it has empty position. So, insert 4 over there.

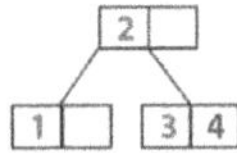

### Insert 5

Element 5 is larger than root node 2. It is not a leaf node so move towards right. we reach a leaf node but it is already full. So, split that node by sending the middle value 4 to the parent node 2. There is an empty position in the parent node. So, element 4 is added with the root node and 5 is added as new leaf node.

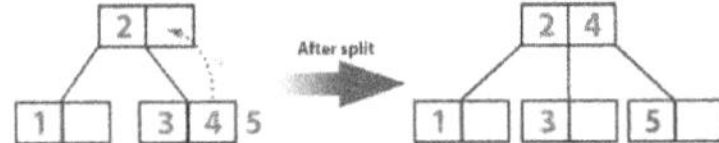

### Insert 6

Element 6 is greater than 2 & 4 and it is not a leaf node. So, move to right of it and there is an empty position. Insert 6 at the empty position near 5.

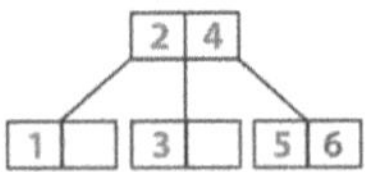

## *Insert 7*

Element 7 is greater than 2 & 4. It is not a leaf node. So, move to the right of 4 and there is leaf node which is already full. So, we split that node by sending middle value 6 to the parent node 2 & 4 but it is also already full.So, again split the node 2 & 4 by sending the middle value 4 to its parent but this node doesn't have parent. So, the element 4 becomes new root node for the tree.

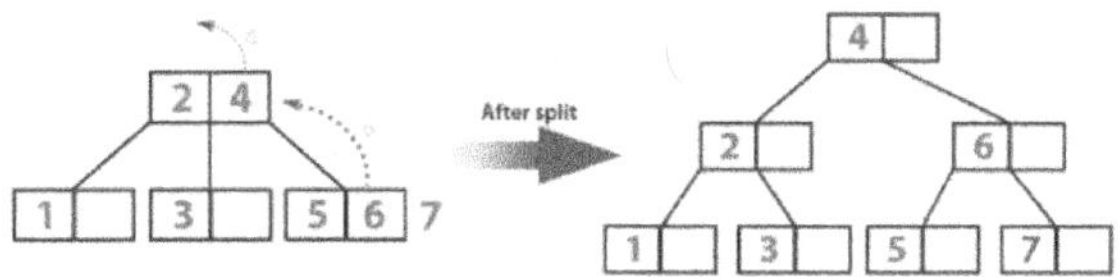


## *Insert 8*

Element 8 is larger than root node 4 and it is not a leaf node. So, move to the right of 4 and we reach a node with value 6.8 is larger than 6 and it is also not a leaf node. So, move to the right of 6 and we reach a leaf node 7 and it has an empty position. So, new element 8 can be inserted at that empty position.

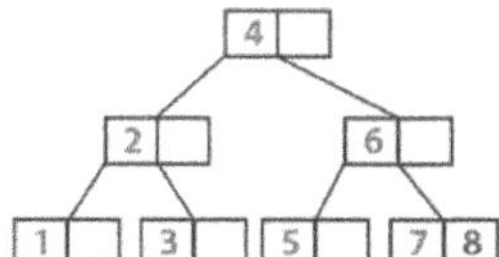

## *Insert 9*

Elemet 9 is larger than root node 4 and it is not a leaf node.So, we move to the right of 4.we reach a node with value 6 and 9 is larger then 6 and it is also not a leaf node.So, we move to the right of 6 and we reach the leaf node 7 & 8.It is already full.So, split this node by sending the middle value 8 to its patrent node.The parent node 6 has an empty position. So, 8 is added at that position.

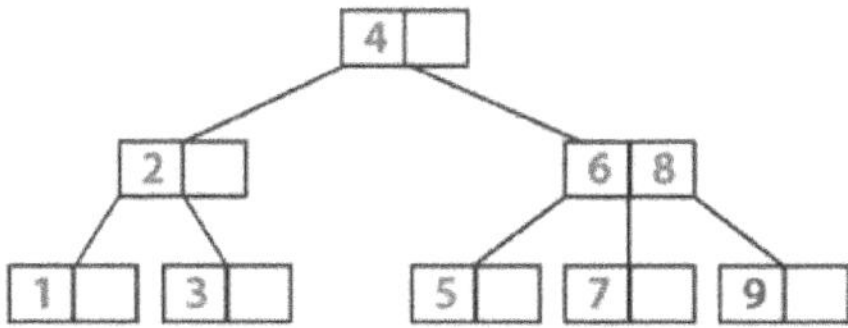

## *Insert 10*

Element 10 is larger than root node 4 and it is not a leaf node.So, move to the right of 4 and we reach a node with value 6 & 8.10 is larger than 6 & 8 amd it is not a leaf node.So, move to right of 8.we reach a leaf node 9 and it has an empty position.So, new element 10 is added at that empty position.

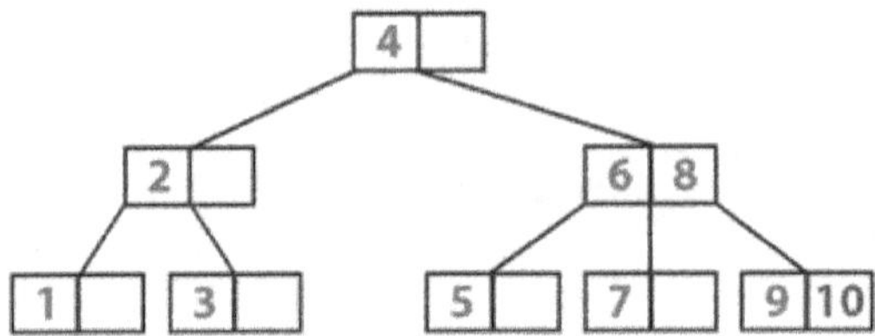

# HASHING

Hashing is an effective way to reduce the number of comparisons. A Hash table or Hash map is a data structure that associates key with values. Any large information source (data base) can be thought of as a table (with multiple fields) containing information.

Ex: Telephone Directory.

## 6.1. Hash Table

It is a data structure used for storing and retrieving data very quickly. It is an array of some fixed size containing the keys. A **hash table** is a collection of items which are stored in such a way as to make it easy to find them later. Each position of the hash table, often called a slot, can hold an item and is named by an integer value starting at 0. For example, we will have a slot named 0, a slot named 1, a slot named 2, and so on. Initially, the hash table contains no items so every slot is empty.Fig shows a hash table of size m=11. In other words, there are *m* slots in the table, named 0 through 10.

| None | None | None | None | None | None | None | None | None | None | None |
|------|------|------|------|------|------|------|------|------|------|------|
| 0 | 1 | 2 | 3 | 4 | 5 | 6 | 7 | 8 | 9 | 10 |

## 6.2. Hash Function

It is used to put data into the hash table.one can use the same hash function to retrieve the data from the hash table. The mapping between an item and the slot where that item belongs in the hash table is called the **hash function**. The hash function will take any item in the collection and return an integer in the range of slot names, between 0 and $m$-1. Assume that we have the set of integer items 54, 26, 93, 17, 77, and 31. Our first hash function, sometimes referred to as the "remainder method," simply takes an item and divides it by the table size, returning the remainder as its hash value (h(item)=item%11). Table gives all of the hash values for our example items. Note that this remainder method (modulo arithmetic) will typically be present in some form in all hash functions, since the result must be in the range of slot names.

| Item | Hash value |
|------|------------|
| 54 | 10 |
| 26 | 4 |
| 93 | 5 |
| 17 | 6 |
| 77 | 0 |
| 31 | 9 |

Once the hash values have been computed, we can insert each item into the hash table at the designated position as shown in Fig below. Note that 6 of the 11 slots are now occupied. This is referred to as the **load factor**, and is commonly denoted by $\lambda$=number of items/table size. For this example, $\lambda=6/11$

| 77 | None | None | None | 26 | 93 | 17 | None | None | 31 | 54 |
|----|------|------|------|----|----|----|------|------|----|----|
| 0 | 1 | 2 | 3 | 4 | 5 | 6 | 7 | 8 | 9 | 10 |

**Hash key:** The integer returned by the hash function.

A simple hash function is

$$hash\ key = key\ mod\ table\text{-}size.$$

Ex: hash (25) = 75 mod 10 = 5

The key value 75 is placed in the relative location 5.

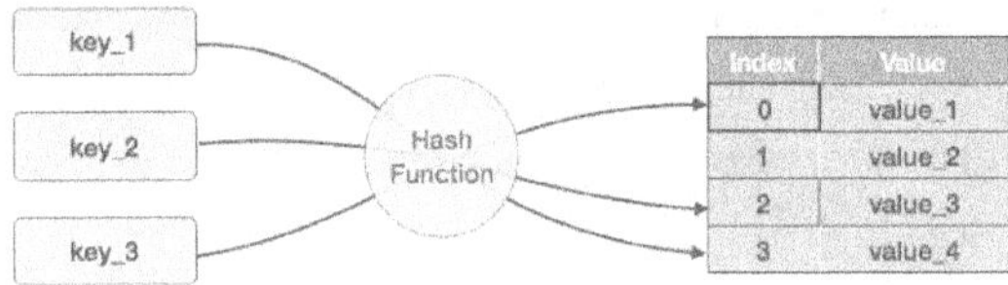

Consider an example of hash table of size 20, and the following items are to be stored. Item are in the (key, value) format. (1,20) , (2,70) , (42,80) ,(4,25) , (12,44) , (14,32)

| S.No | Key | Hash | Array Index |
|------|-----|------|-------------|
| 1 | 1 | 1%20=1 | 1 |
| 2 | 2 | 2%20=2 | 2 |
| 3 | 42 | 42%20=2 | 2 |
| 4 | 4 | 4%20=4 | 4 |
| 5 | 12 | 12%20=12 | 12 |
| 6 | 14 | 14%20=14 | 14 |

## 6.3.    Types of Hash Function

### 1. *Division Method*

The hash function depends upon the remainder of division.It is always better to select table size not close to power of 2.

H(Key)=return key % Table_Size

Ex: 54, 72, 89, 37

Table size=10

| 0 | 1 | 2 | 3 | 4 | 5 | 6 | 7 | 8 | 9 |
|---|---|---|---|---|---|---|---|---|---|
|  |  | 72 |  | 54 |  |  | 37 |  | 89 |

## 2. Mid Square

In the mid square method, the key is squared and the middle part of the result is used as index. This method works if the keys do not contain a lot of leading or trailing zeros.

$$H(X) = \text{return middle digits of } X^2$$

Ex: $3111=3111^2=9678321$

Table size=1000

H(3111)=782(middle of 3 digits).

## 3. Digit Folding

The key is divided into separate parts and using some simple operation these parts are combined to produce the hash value.

Ex:12365412

H(key)=123+654+12=789

The record is placed at the location 789.

## 6.4.   Collision

This technique is going to work only if each item maps to a unique location in the hash table. For example, if the item 44 had been the next item in our collection, it would have a hash value of 0 (40%10==0). Since 70 also had a hash value of 0, we would have a problem. According to the hash function, two or more items would need to be in the same slot. This is referred to as a collision (it may also be called a "clash"). Clearly, collisions create a problem for the hashing technique.

Ex: 11, 23, 33, 55, 63

11%10=0

23%10=3

33%10=3   already 3rd position occupied so place 33 at 4th place

55%10=3

63%10=3   already 3rd, 4th and 5thposition occupied so place 63 at 6th position

| 0 | 1 | 2 | 3 | 4 | 5 | 6 | 7 | 8 | 9 |
|---|---|---|---|---|---|---|---|---|---|
|   | 11 |   | 23 | 33 | 55 | 63 |   |   |   |

Collisions can be reduced with a selection of a good hash function. But it is not possible to avoid collisions altogether

- Unless we can find a perfect hash function
- Which is hard to do

## 6.5.   Collision Resolving Strategies

Few Collision Resolution ideas

- Separate chaining

Some Open addressing techniques

- Linear Probing
- Quadratic Probing

### 6.5.1.  Separate Chaining

Collisions can be resolved by creating a list of keys that map to the same value. It is a collision resolution technique to overcome the disadvantage of open addressing. Handling of overflow records is done by having a special chained feature called overflow area and prime area.

The area contains the path of the table into which records are initially hashed (prime area). A separate linked list is maintained for each set of colliding records (Overflow area).

A pointer field is required for each record in the prime and overflow area.

The colliding record in each linked list are not kept in alphabetical order.

When a new colliding record is entered in the overflowing area it is placed in the front of those records in the appropriate linked list in the overflow area.

Overflow area is a linked list and hence it grows on and hence no overflow. Here searching is inefficient.

## Example

Let us consider a simple hash function as "**key mod 7**" and sequence of keys as 50, 700, 76, 85, 92, 73, 101.

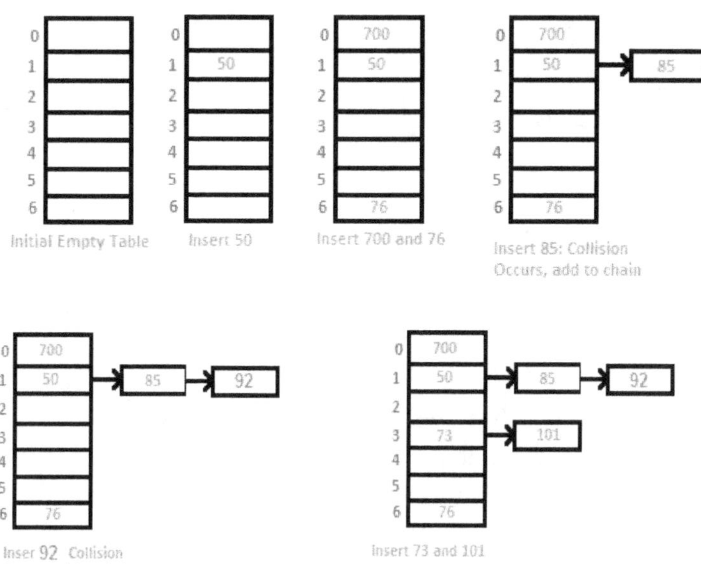


## Advantages

a.  Simple to implement.

b.  Hash table never fills up, we can always add more elements to chain.

c.  Less sensitive to the hash function or load factors.

d.  It is mostly used when it is unknown how many and how frequently keys may be inserted or deleted.

## Disadvantages

1.  Cache performance of chaining is not good as keys are stored using linked list. Open addressing provides better cache performance as everything is stored in same table.

2.  Wastage of Space (Some Parts of hash table are never used)

3.  If the chain becomes long, then search time can become O(n) in worst case.

4.  Uses extra space for links

### *Program*

```c
#include <stdio.h>
#include<stdlib.h>
#define MAX 20
struct Employee
{
int employee_id;
char employee_name[45];
int employee_age;
};
struct Record
{
struct Employee data;
struct Record *link;
};
void insert(struct Employee employee_record, struct Record *hash_table[]);
int search_element(int key, struct Record *hash_table[]);
void remove_record(int key, struct Record *hash_table[]);
void show(struct Record *hash_table[]);
int hash_function(int key);
int main()
{
struct Record *hash_table[MAX];
struct Employee employee_record;
int count, key, option;
for(count = 0; count <= MAX - 1; count++)
{
hash_table[count] = NULL;
}
while(1)
{
printf("1. Insert a Record in Hash Table\n");
printf("2. Search for a Record\n");
printf("3. Delete a Record\n");
```

```c
printf("4. Show Hash Table\n");
printf("5. Quit\n");
printf("Enter your option\n");
scanf("%d",&option);
switch(option)
{
case 1 :
printf("Enter the Employee Details\n");
printf("Employee ID:\t");
scanf("%d", &employee_record.employee_id);
printf("Employee Name:\t");
scanf("%s", employee_record.employee_name);
printf("Employee Age:\t");
scanf("%d", &employee_record.employee_age);
insert(employee_record, hash_table);
break;
case 2 :
printf("Enter the element to search:\t");
scanf("%d", &key);
count = search_element(key, hash_table);
if(count == -1)
{
printf("Element Not Found\n");
}
else
{
printf("Element Found in Chain:\t%d\n", count);
}
break;
case 3:
printf("Enter the element to delete:\t");
scanf("%d", &key);
remove_record(key, hash_table);
break;
```

```c
case 4:
show(hash_table);
break;
case 5:
exit(1);
}
}
return 0;
}
void insert(struct Employee employee_record, struct Record *hash_table[])
{
int key, h;
struct Record *temp;
key = employee_record.employee_id;
if(search_element(key, hash_table) != -1)
{
printf("Duplicate Key\n");
return;
}
    h = hash_function(key);
temp = malloc(sizeof(struct Record));
temp->data = employee_record;
temp->link = hash_table[h];
hash_table[h] = temp;
}
void show(struct Record *hash_table[])
{
int count;
struct Record *ptr;
for(count = 0; count < MAX; count++)
{
printf("\n[%3d]", count);
if(hash_table[count] != NULL)
{
```

```c
ptr = hash_table[count];
while(ptr != NULL)
{
printf("%d %s %d\t", ptr->data.employee_id, ptr->data.employee_name, ptr-
>data.employee_age);
ptr=ptr->link;
}
}
}
printf("\n");
}
int search_element(int key, struct Record *hash_table[])
{
int h;
struct Record *ptr;
h = hash_function(key);
ptr = hash_table[h];
while(ptr != NULL)
{
if(ptr->data.employee_id == key)
{
return h;
}
ptr = ptr->link;
}
return -1;
}
void remove_record(int key, struct Record *hash_table[])
{
int h;
   struct Record *temp, *ptr;
h = hash_function(key);
if(hash_table[h]==NULL)
{
```

```c
printf("Key %d Not Found\n", key);
return;
}
if(hash_table[h]->data.employee_id == key)
{
temp = hash_table[h];
hash_table[h] = hash_table[h]->link;
free(temp);
return;
}
ptr = hash_table[h];
while(ptr->link != NULL)
{
if(ptr->link->data.employee_id == key)
{
temp = ptr->link;
ptr->link = temp->link;
free(temp);
return;
}
ptr = ptr->link;
}
printf("Key %d Not Found\n", key);
}
int hash_function(int key)
{
return (key % MAX);
}
```

### 6.5.2.  *Open Addressing*

### *Linear Probing*

One method for resolving collisions looks into the hash table and tries to find another open slot to hold the item that caused the collision. A simple way to do this is to start at the original hash value position and then move in a sequential manner through the slots until we encounter the first slot that is empty. Note that we may need to go back to the first slot (circularly) to cover the entire hash table. This collision resolution process is referred to as **open addressing** in that it tries to find the next open slot or address in the hash table. By systematically visiting each slot one at a time, we are performing an open addressing technique called **linear probing.**

## *Example 1*

Set of hash codes consisting of {89, 18, 49, 58, 9} and we need to place them into a table of size 10.

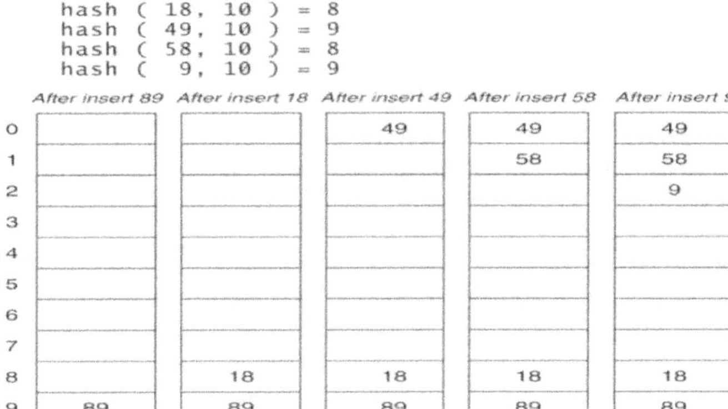


## *Example 2*

Let us consider a simple hash function as "key mod 7" and sequence of keys as 50, 700, 76, 85, 92, 73, 101.

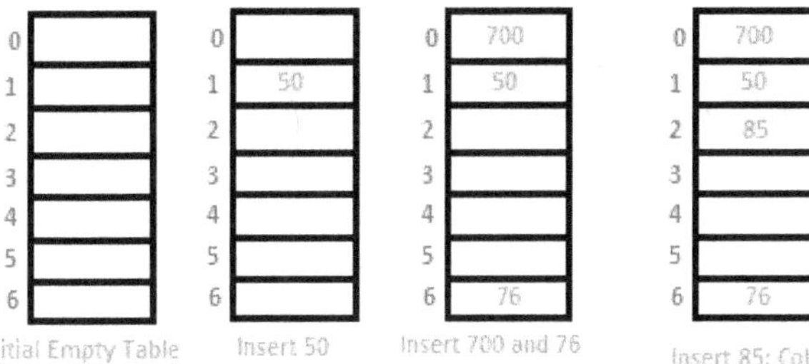

The first collision occurs when 49 hashes to the same location with index 9. Since 89 occupies the A[9], we need to place 49 to the next available position. Considering the array as circular, the next available position is 0. That is (9+1) mod 10. So we place 49 in A[0]. Several more collisions occur in this simple example and in each case, we keep looking to find the next available location in the array to place the element. Now if we need to find the element, say for example, 49, we first compute the hash code (9), and look in A[9]. Since we do not find it there, we look in A[(9+1) % 10] = A[0], we find it there and we are done. So what if we are looking for 79? First we compute hashcode of 79 = 9. We probe in A[9], A[(9+1)%10]=A[0], A[(9+2)%10]=A[1], A[(9+3)%10]=A[2], A[(9+4)%10]=A[3] etc. Since A[3] = null, we do know that 79 could not exists in the set.

## Algorithm

Step 1: calculate the initial position using a hash function.

Step 2: Repeat step 4 to examine all the locations in the table.

Step 3: If the current location contains the key, then if not inserting into the table then return position of the record else return in insertion.

Step 4: If the current location is empty or has a deleted value then if inserting into the table then insert the record and return its position else if the location is empty then return error.

Step 5: Write overflow error.

## Difficulties in Open Addressing

i. List of colliding records for different hash values become intermixed.

ii. Unable to handle overflow situation in a satisfactory manner.

iii. On deleting an overflow, the entire table must be reorganised.

### Program

```c
#include<stdio.h>
void main()
{
int a[10]={1,2,3,4,5,6,7,8,9,10};
int n,value;
int temp, hash;
clrscr();
printf("\nEnter the value of n(table size):");
scanf("%d",&n);
do
{
printf("\nEnter the hash value");
scanf("%d",&value);
hash=value%n;
if(a[hash]==0)
{
a[hash]=value;
printf("\na[%d]the value %d is stored",hash,value);
}
else
{
for(hash++;hash<n;hash++)
{
if(a[hash]==0)
{
printf("Space is allocated give other value");
a[hash]=value;
printf("\n a[%d]the value %d is stored",hash,value);
goto menu;
}
}
hash=0;
for(hash;hash<n;hash++)
```

```c
{
if(a[hash]==0)
{
printf("Space is allocated give other value");
a[hash]=value;
printf("\n a[%d]the value %d is stored",hash,value);
goto menu;
}
}
printf("ERROR");
printf("\nEnter '0' and press 'Enter key' twice to exit");
}
menu:
printf("\n Do u want enter more");
scanf("%d",&temp);
}
while(temp==1);
getch();}
```

# CHAPTER 7

# GRAPHS

## 7.1.  Introduction

Graph is a non-linear data structure, it contains a set of points known as nodes (or vertices) and set of links known as edges (or Arcs) which connects the vertices. A graph is defined as follows

- Graph is a collection of vertices and arcs which connects vertices in the graph.
- Graph is a collection of nodes and edges which connects nodes in the graph.
- Generally, a graph G is represented as G = (V, E), where V is set of vertices and E is set of edges.

### *Example*

The following is a graph with 5 vertices and 6 edges.

This graph G can be defined as G = {V, E}

Where V = {A, B, C, D, E} and E = {(A,B),(A,C)(A,D),(B,D),(C,D),(B,E),(E,D)}.

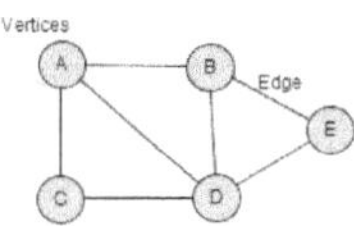


## 7.2.  Graph Terminology

### *1.  Directed Graph*

A directed graph or digraph is a pair G = {V, E}, where each edge in E is unidirectional. It is also called as one-way graph.

$$(v, w) \neq (w, v)$$

The number of possible edges in a directed graph is $n^2$

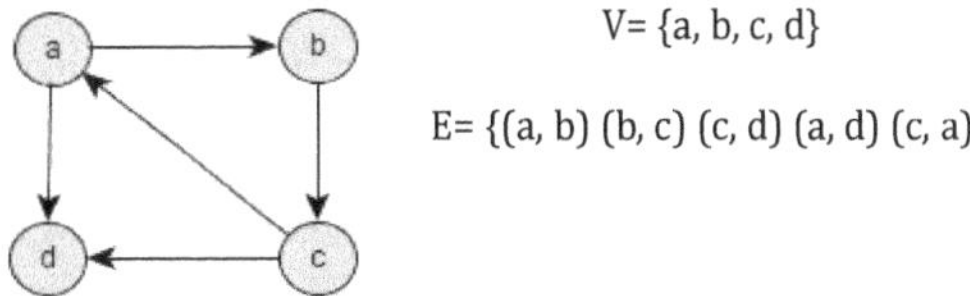


V= {a, b, c, d}

E= {(a, b) (b, c) (c, d) (a, d) (c, a)}

## 2. *Undirected Graph*

An undirected graph is a graph which consists of undirected edges. The number of possible edges in an Undirected graph is n(n-1)/2.

$$(v, w) = (w, v)$$

Ex. Airline route map

Possible Edges=3(3-1)/2

6/2=3

V= {v1, v2,v3}

E= {(v1,v2) (v2,v3) (v1,v3)}

## 3. *Weighted Graph*

If every edge in the graph is assigned a value it is called as weighted graph. It can be directed or undirected graph.

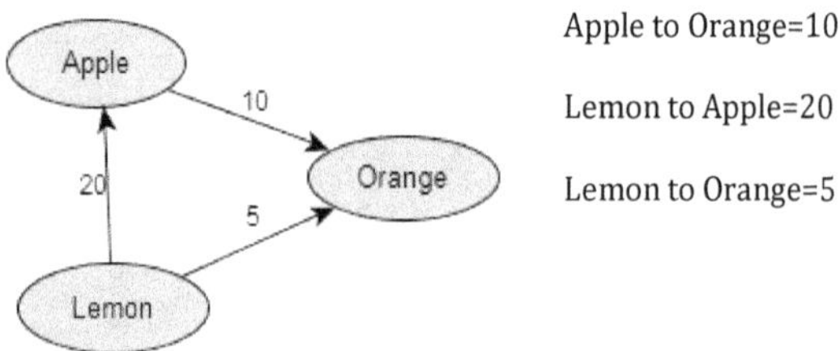

Apple to Orange=10

Lemon to Apple=20

Lemon to Orange=5

## 4. *Complete Graph*

A Complete Graph is a graph in which there is an edge between every pair of vertices. A complete graph with n vertices will have n(n-1)/2 edges.It is usually undirected graph.

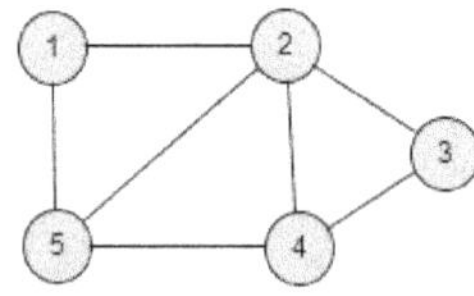

## 5. *Strongly Connected Graph*

If there is a path from every vertex to every other vertex in a directed graph, it is strongly connected graph.

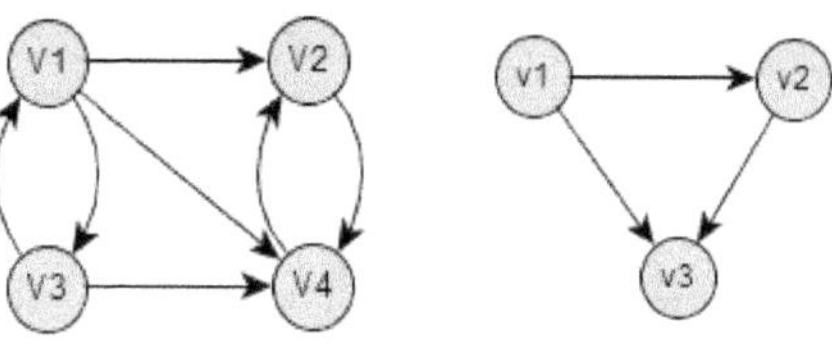


## 6. *Path*

A path is a sequence of alternating vertices and edges that starts at a vertex and ends at a vertex such that each edge is incident to its predecessor and successor vertex. Path length from vertex V to itself is zero.

Length of path = Number of edge traversed.  Path from a to f = 3

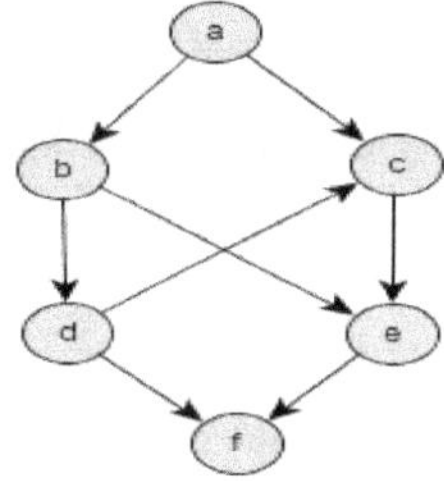


## 7. *Loop*

If the graph contains an edge (v, v) from a vertex to itself, then it is loop.

## 8. *Cycle*

A cycle in a graph is a path in which first and last vertex are the same.

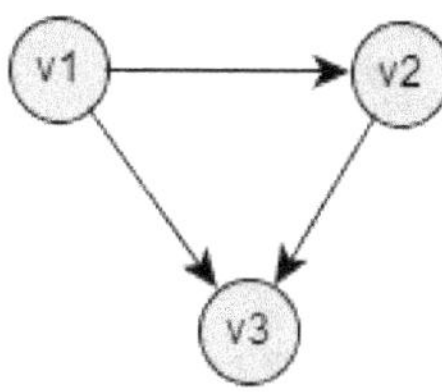


A graph which has cycles is referred to as cyclic graph.

## 9. *Acyclic Graph*

A directed graph which has no cycles. It is abbreviated as DAG (Directed Acyclic Graph)

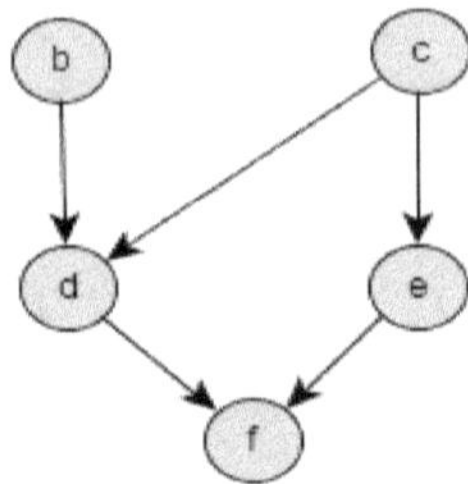


## 10. *Degree*

The number of edges incident on a vertex determines its degree (v).

- The **indegree** of vertex v is the number of edges entering into the vertex v.
- The **Outdegree** of vertex v is the number of edges existing from vertex v.

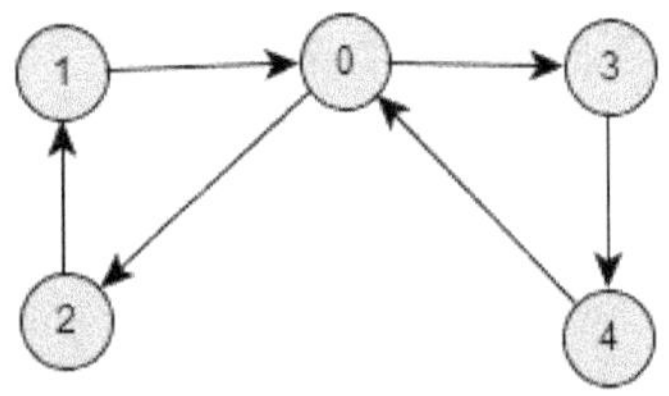


Indegree (0) = 2, Outdegree (0) = 2

Indegree (1) = 1, Outdegree (0) = 1

Indegree (2) = 1, Outdegree (0) = 1

Indegree (3) = 1, Outdegree (0) = 1

Indegree (4) = 1, Outdegree (0) = 1

## 7.3.  Representation of Graph

Graph data structure is represented using following representations

1. Adjacency Matrix
2. Adjacency List

## 1. *Adjacency Matrix*

In this representation, graph can be represented using a matrix of size total number of vertices by total number of vertices. That means if a graph with 5 vertices can be represented using a matrix of 5X5 class. In this matrix, rows and columns both represents vertices. This matrix is filled with either 1 or 0. Here, 1 represents there is an edge from row vertex to column vertex and 0 represents there is no edge from row vertex to column vertex. For example, consider the following undirected graph representation

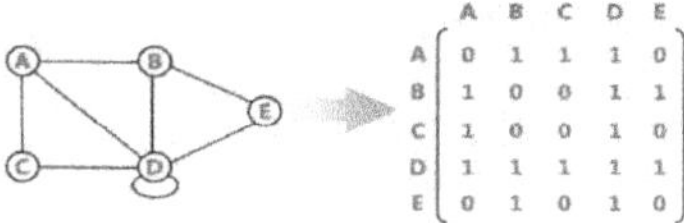

Directed graph representation.

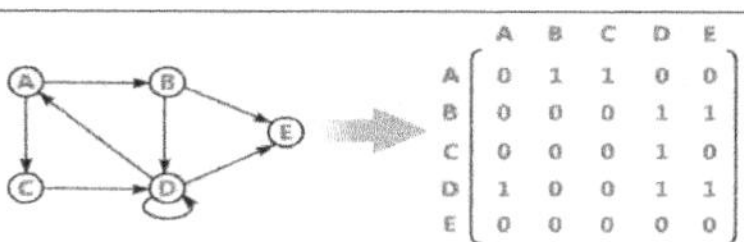

## 2. Adjacency List

In this representation, every vertex of graph contains list of its adjacent vertices. For example, consider the following directed graph representation implemented using linked list.

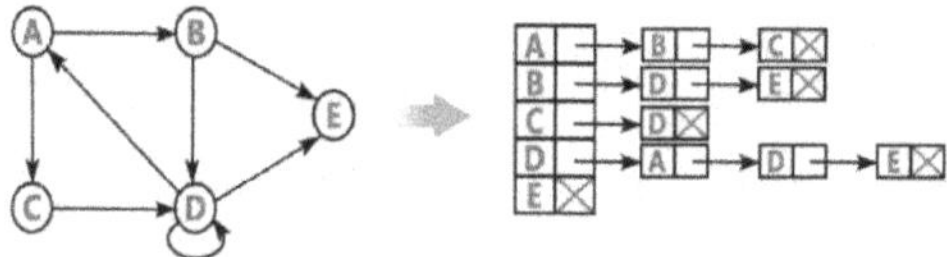

This representation can also be implemented using array as follows.

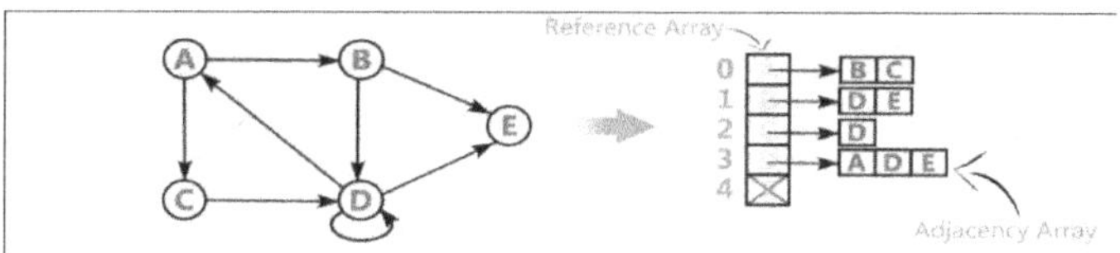

## 7.4. Topological Sort

Topological sorting for Directed Acyclic Graph (DAG) is a linear ordering of vertices such that for every directed edge uv, vertex u comes before v in the ordering. Topological Sorting for a graph is not possible if the graph is not a DAG.

### Algorithm

1. Assume Indegree is stored with each node.
2. Repeat until no nodes remain

   Choose a node of zero indegree and output it (Dequeue)

   Remove the node and all its edges and update indegree.

### *Routine*

```
Void topological(graph G)
{
queue  Q;
int counter = 0;
vertex v,w;
Q= CreateQueue(NumVertex);
MakeEmpty(Q);
for each vertex v
      if (indegree[v] = = 0)
                Enqueue(v,Q);
while(!isEmpty(Q))
{
V=Dequeue (Q);
TopNum[v]= ++Counter;
for  each w adjacent to v
      if(--indegree[w] = = 0)
                Enqueue(w,Q);
}
if (counter != Numvetrex)
      Error("Graph has a cycle");
DisposeQueue(Q);
```

### *Example*

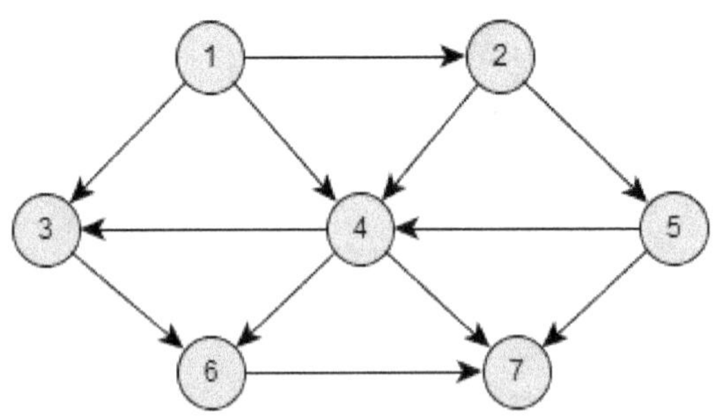

| Vertex | 1 | 2 | 3 | 4 | 5 | 6 | 7 | 1 |
|---|---|---|---|---|---|---|---|---|
| V1 | 0 | 0 | 0 | 0 | 0 | 0 | 0 | 0 |
| V2 | 1 | 0 | 0 | 0 | 0 | 0 | 0 | 1 |
| V3 | 2 | 1 | 1 | 1 | 0 | 0 | 0 | 2 |
| V4 | 3 | 2 | 1 | 0 | 0 | 0 | 0 | 3 |
| V5 | 1 | 1 | 0 | 0 | 0 | 0 | 0 | 1 |
| V6 | 3 | 3 | 3 | 3 | 2 | 1 | 0 | 3 |
| V7 | 2 | 2 | 2 | 1 | 0 | 0 | 0 | 2 |
| Enqueue | V1 | V2 | V5 | V4 | V3, V7 | | V6 | V1 |
| Dequeue | V1 | V2 | V5 | V4 | V3 | V7 | V6 | V1 |

## 7.5. Shortest Path Algorithm

The shortest path problem is about finding a path between 2 vertices in a graph such that the total sum of the edges weights is minimum. There are 4 versions of problem

- unweighted shortest path
- weighted shortest path with positive edges
- weighted shortest path with negative edges
- weighted Acyclic graph

### 7.5.1. Unweighted Shortest Path

In an unweighted graph, breadth-first search guarantees that when we first make it to a node $v$. we can be sure we have found the shortest path to it; more searching will never find a path to $v$ with fewer edges.

### Algorithm

1. Create a queue, where the size of the queue is equivalent to the number of vertices of the graph.
2. Empty the Queue.
3. Select a source vertex(S) and insert the source vertex (S) into the queue.
4. Find the unknown vertices adjacent to source vertex (S) and update the distance (dv)

| Known | dv | pv |
|---|---|---|
| Variable | Distance | Vertex from s to v |

5. Repeat step 4 until all the vertices in graph G are found to be known and gets processed.

### *Routine*

Void unweighted (Table T)

{

int currdist;

vertex V,W;

for(currdist=0;currdist<numvetex;currdist++)

for each vertex V

if(!T[V].known && T[V]==currdist)

{

T[V].known=True;

for each W adjacent to V

if(T[W].dist==infinity)

{

T[W].dist=currdist+1;

T[W].path=V;}

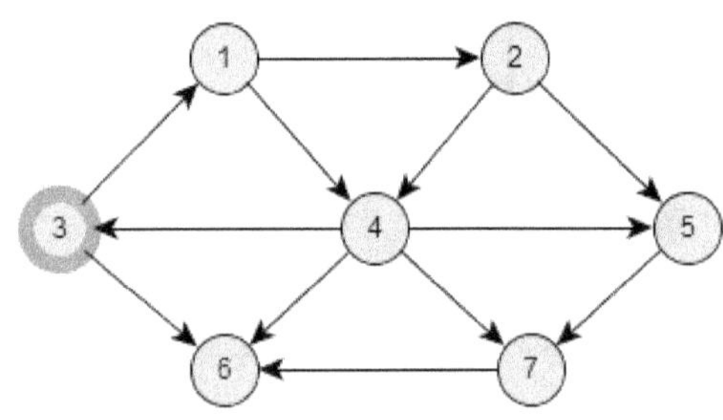



*Out degree*

V3->v1, v6

V1->v2, v4

V6-> -

V2->v1, v4, v5

V4->v3, v5, v6, v7

V5->v7

V7->v6

| vertex | Initial State | | | V3 | | | V1 | | | V6 | | |
|---|---|---|---|---|---|---|---|---|---|---|---|---|
| | Known | dv | pv | Known | dv | pv | Known | dv | pv | Known | dv | pv |
| V1 | 0 | ∞ | 0 | 0 | 1 | V3 | 1 | 1 | V3 | 1 | 1 | V3 |
| V2 | 0 | ∞ | 0 | 0 | ∞ | 0 | 0 | 2 | V1 | 0 | 2 | V1 |
| V3 | 0 | 0 | 0 | 1 | 0 | 0 | 1 | 0 | 0 | 1 | 0 | 0 |
| V4 | 0 | ∞ | 0 | 0 | ∞ | 0 | 0 | 2 | V1 | 0 | 2 | V1 |
| V5 | 0 | ∞ | 0 | 0 | ∞ | 0 | 0 | ∞ | 0 | 0 | ∞ | 0 |
| V6 | 0 | ∞ | 0 | 0 | 1 | V3 | 0 | 1 | V3 | 1 | 1 | V3 |
| V7 | 0 | ∞ | 0 | 0 | ∞ | 0 | 0 | ∞ | 0 | 0 | ∞ | 0 |
| Enqueue | V3 | | | V1, V6 | | | V6, V2, V4 | | | V2, V4 | | |

| Vertex | V2 | | | V4 | | | V5 | | | V7 | | |
|---|---|---|---|---|---|---|---|---|---|---|---|---|
|  | Known | dv | pv | Known | dv | pv | Known | dv | pv | Known | dv | pv |
| V1 | 1 | 1 | V3 | 1 | 1 | V3 | 1 | 1 | V3 | 1 | 1 | V3 |
| V2 | 0 | 2 | V1 | 1 | 2 | V1 | 1 | 2 | V1 | 1 | 2 | V1 |
| V3 | 1 | 0 | 0 | 1 | 0 | 0 | 1 | 0 | 0 | 1 | 0 | 0 |
| V4 | 0 | 2 | V1 | 1 | 2 | V1 | 1 | 2 | V1 | 1 | 2 | V1 |
| V5 | 0 | 3 | V2 | 0 | 3 | V2 | 1 | 3 | V2 | 1 | 3 | V2 |
| V6 | 1 | 1 | V3 | 1 | 1 | V3 | 1 | 1 | V3 | 1 | 1 | V3 |
| V7 | 0 | $\infty$ | 0 | 0 | 3 | V4 | 0 | 3 | V4 | 1 | 3 | V4 |
| Enqueue | V4, V5 | | | V5 | | | V7 | | | Empty | | |

Solution: V3, V1, V6, V2, V4, V5, V7

### 7.5.2. *Weighted Shortest Path Algorithms*

### 7.5.2.a *Dijkstra's Algorithm*

It is applied on weighted graph to find the single source shortest path in the graph, by using the same technique as that of unweighted graphs.

It picks the unvisited vertex with the lowest distance, calculates the distance through it to each unvisited neighbour, and updates the neighbour's distance if smaller.

It was discovered by Edsger W. Dijkstra in 1956

### *Algorithm*

- Assign to every node a tentative distance value, set it to zero for our initial node and to infinity for all other nodes.
- Set the initial node as current. Mark all other nodes unvisited. Create a set of all the unvisited nodes called the unvisited set.
- Calculate the distance(dv) for outdegree nodes of source node(A) and mark the current node as visited and remove it from the unvisited set. A visited node will never be checked again.
- If the destination node has been marked visited (when planning a route between two specific nodes) or if the smallest tentative distance among the nodes in the unvisited set is infinity (when planning a complete traversal; occurs when there is no connection between the initial node and remaining unvisited nodes), then stop. The algorithm has finished.

### Routine

```
Void Dijkstra(Table T)
{
vertex V, W;
for(;;)
{
V=smallest unknown distance vertex;
if(V==NotAVertex)
break;
T[V].known=True;
for each W adjacent to V
if(!T[W].known)
if(T[V].dist+Cvw<T[W].dist)
{
Decrease (T[W].dist to T[V].Dist+Cvw);
T[W].path=V
}
}
}
```

### Example

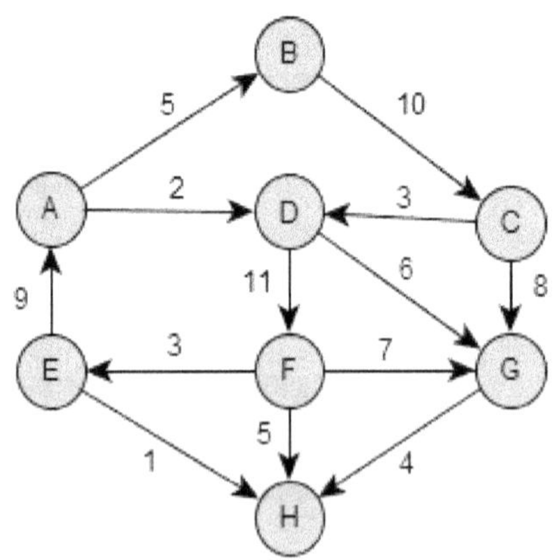

| Vertex | A | | | D | | | B | | | G | | |
|---|---|---|---|---|---|---|---|---|---|---|---|---|
| | Known | dv | pv | Known | dv | pv | Known | dv | pv | Known | dv | pv |
| A | 1 | 0 | 0 | 1 | 0 | 0 | 1 | 0 | 0 | 1 | 0 | 0 |
| B | 0 | 5 | A | 0 | 5 | A | 1 | 5 | A | 1 | 5 | A |
| C | 0 | ∞ | 0 | 0 | ∞ | 0 | 0 | 15 | B | 0 | 15 | B |
| D | 0 | 2 | A | 1 | 2 | A | 1 | 2 | A | 1 | 2 | A |
| E | 0 | ∞ | 0 | 0 | ∞ | 0 | 0 | ∞ | 0 | 0 | ∞ | 0 |
| F | 0 | ∞ | 0 | 0 | 13 | D | 0 | 13 | D | 0 | 13 | D |
| G | 0 | ∞ | 0 | 0 | 8 | D | 0 | 8 | D | 1 | 8 | D |
| H | 0 | ∞ | 0 | 0 | ∞ | 0 | 0 | ∞ | 0 | 0 | 12 | G |

| Vertex | H | | | F | | | C | | | E | | |
|---|---|---|---|---|---|---|---|---|---|---|---|---|
| | Known | dv | pv | Known | dv | pv | Known | dv | pv | Known | dv | pv |
| A | 1 | 0 | 0 | 1 | 0 | 0 | 1 | 0 | 0 | 1 | 0 | 0 |
| B | 1 | 5 | A | 1 | 5 | A | 1 | 5 | A | 1 | 5 | A |
| C | 0 | 15 | B | 0 | 15 | B | 1 | 15 | B | 1 | 15 | B |
| D | 1 | 2 | A | 1 | 2 | A | 1 | 2 | A | 1 | 2 | A |
| E | 0 | ∞ | 0 | 0 | 16 | F | 0 | 16 | F | 1 | 16 | F |
| F | 0 | 13 | D | 1 | 13 | D | 1 | 13 | D | 1 | 13 | D |
| G | 1 | 8 | D | 1 | 8 | D | 1 | 8 | D | 1 | 8 | D |
| H | 1 | 12 | G | 1 | 12 | G | 1 | 12 | G | 1 | 12 | G |

Solution:　　　A->D->B->G->H->F->C->E

## 7.6. Minimum Spanning Tree

A minimum spanning tree (MST) or minimum weight spanning tree is a subset of the edges of a connected, edge-weighted undirected graph that connects all the vertices together, without any cycles and with the minimum possible total edge weight.A minimum spanning tree (MST) exists if and only if G is connected. The number of edges in the MST is (I v I -1). It is a tree because it is cyclic, it is spanning because it covers every vertex, and it is minimum becauseit covers minimum cost.

Example:　　Number of Vertices = 4

　　　　　　Possible Edges = 3 (v -1)

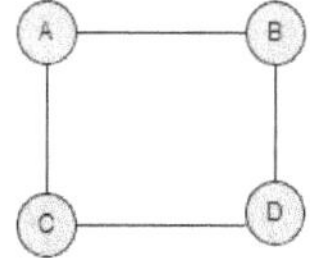

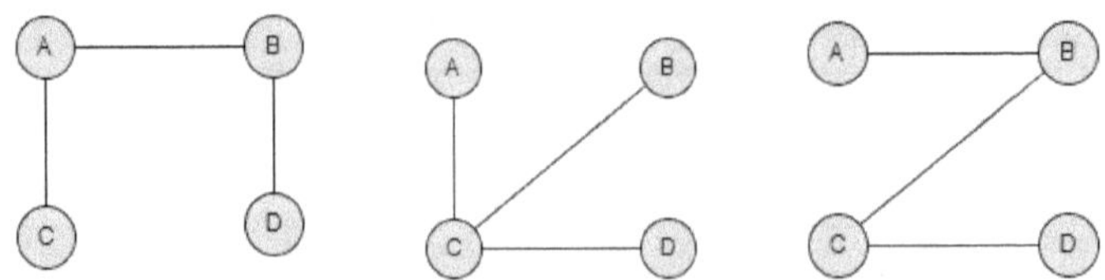

Minimum spanning tree (MST) can be solved using Greedy technique. That is the greedy method selects an input at each stage which derives a feasible solution then it is added to the optimal solution until the problem terminates with a condition.

## Types

- Prim's Algorithm
- Kruskal's algorithm

## Applications

1. wiring a house with a minimum of cable
2. Cheapest cost tour of travelling salesman
3. Networking the Pc's with low cost.

### 7.6.1. Prim's Algorithm

MST is constructed in successive stages.one node is picked as the root and the edge is added i.e., an associated vertex is added to the tree, until all the vertices are present in the tree with (v-1) edges.

## Algorithm

1. One node is picked as a root node(u) from the given connected graph.
2. At each stage choose a new vertex v from u, by considering an edge (u, v) with minimum cost among all edges from u, where u is already in the tree and v is not in the tree.
3. The Prim's algorithm table is constructed with three parameters.

| Known | Vertex is added in the tree |
|-------|------------------------------|
| dv | Weight of the shortest arc |
| pv | Last vertex which causes a change in dv. |

4. After selecting the vertex v, the update rule is applied for each unknown w adjacent to v. The rule is dw=min (dw, (v,w)) that is if more than one path exist between v to w then dw is updated with minimum cost.

## Routine

Void MST-PRIM(G, w, r)

for each u  V [G]

do key[u] ← ∞

π[u] ← NIL

key[r] ← 0

Q ← V [G]

while Q ≠ Ø

do u ← EXTRACT-MIN(Q)

for each v  Adj[u]

do if v  Q and w(u, v) < key[v]

then π[v] ← u

key[v] ← w(u, v)

## Example 1

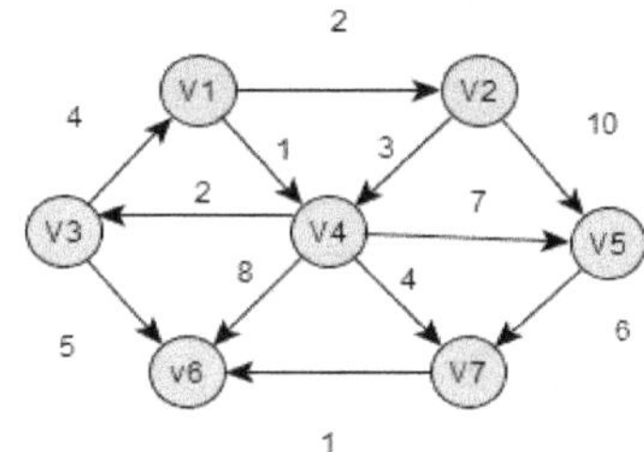

## Steps

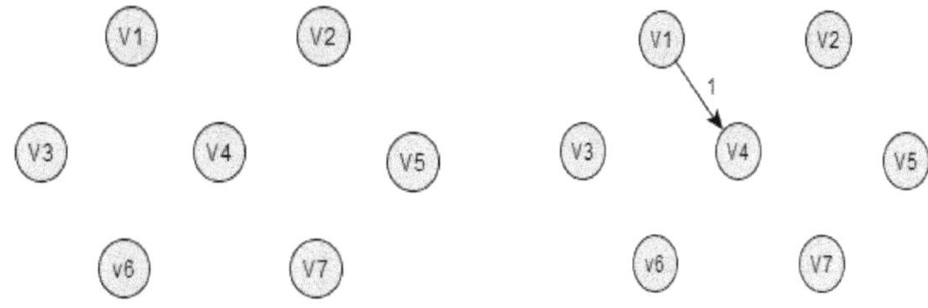

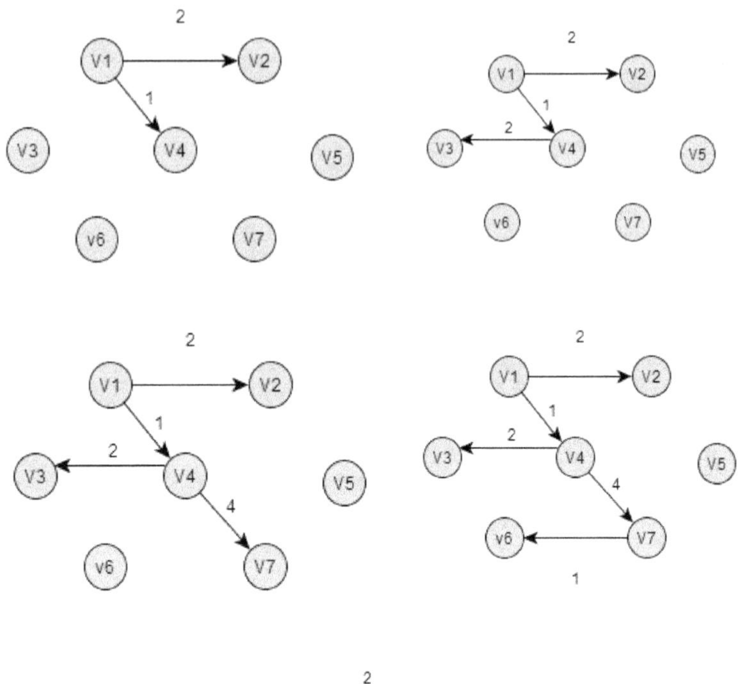

| | V1 | | | V4 | | | V2, V3 | | |
|---|---|---|---|---|---|---|---|---|---|
| Vertex | Known | dv | pv | Known | dv | pv | Known | Dv | pv |
| V1 | 1 | 0 | 0 | 1 | 0 | 0 | 1 | 0 | 0 |
| V2 | 0 | 2 | V1 | 0 | 2 | V1 | 1 | 2 | V1 |
| V3 | 0 | 4 | V1 | 0 | 2 | V4 | 1 | 2 | V4 |
| V4 | 0 | 1 | V1 | 1 | 1 | V1 | 1 | 1 | V1 |
| V5 | 0 | ∞ | 0 | 0 | 7 | V4 | 0 | 7 | V4 |
| V6 | 0 | ∞ | 0 | 0 | 8 | V4 | 0 | 5 | V3 |
| V7 | 0 | ∞ | 0 | 0 | 4 | V4 | 0 | 4 | V4 |

| Vertex | V7 | | | V6 | | | V5 | | |
|---|---|---|---|---|---|---|---|---|---|
| | Known | dv | pv | Known | dv | pv | Known | Dv | Pv |
| V1 | 1 | 0 | 0 | 1 | 0 | 0 | 1 | 0 | 0 |
| V2 | 1 | 2 | V1 | 1 | 2 | V1 | 1 | 2 | V1 |
| V3 | 1 | 2 | V4 | 1 | 2 | V4 | 1 | 2 | V4 |
| V4 | 1 | 1 | V1 | 1 | 1 | V1 | 1 | 1 | V1 |
| V5 | 0 | 6 | V7 | 0 | 6 | V7 | 1 | 6 | V7 |
| V6 | 0 | 1 | V7 | 1 | 1 | V7 | 1 | 1 | V7 |
| V7 | 1 | 4 | V4 | 1 | 4 | V4 | 1 | 4 | V4 |

## *Example 2*

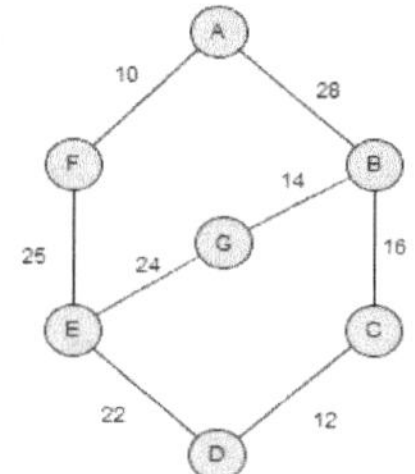

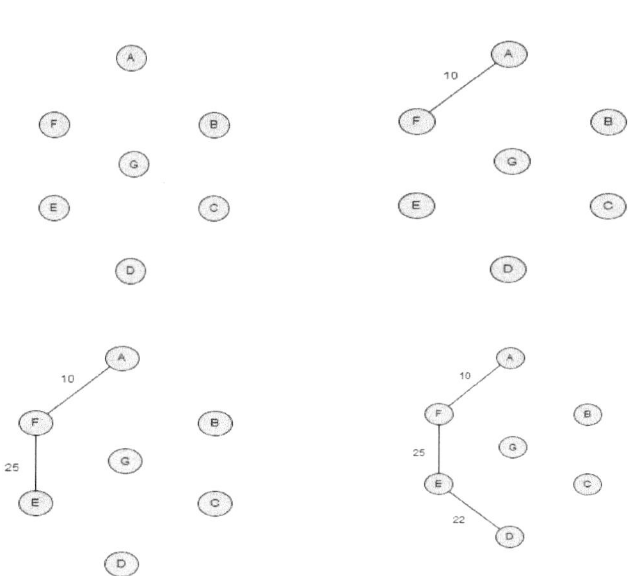

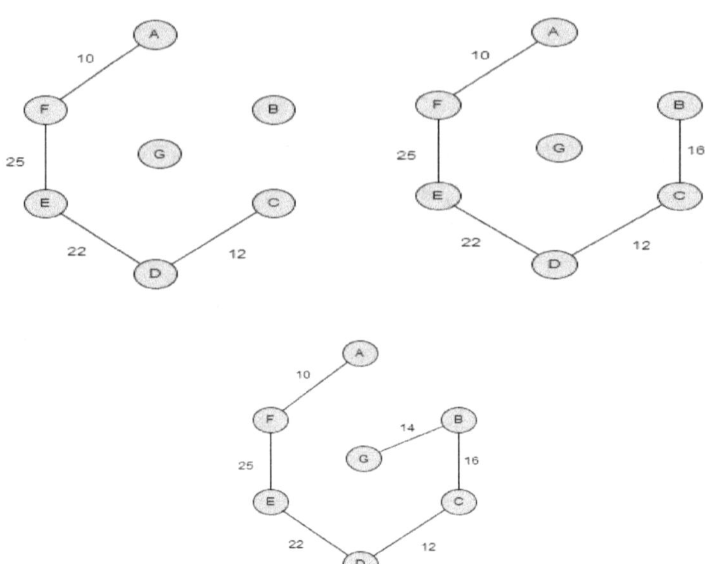

|        | A |  |  | F |  |  | E |  |  |
|--------|-------|-----|-----|-------|-----|-----|-------|-----|-----|
| Vertex | Known | dv | pv | Known | dv | pv | Known | Dv | pv |
| **A** | 1 | 0 | 0 | 1 | 0 | 0 | 1 | 0 | 0 |
| **B** | 0 | 28 | A | 0 | 28 | A | 0 | 28 | A |
| **C** | 0 | ∞ | 0 | 0 | ∞ | 0 | 0 | ∞ | 0 |
| **D** | 0 | ∞ | 0 | 1 | ∞ | 0 | 0 | 22 | E |
| **E** | 0 | ∞ | 0 | 0 | 25 | F | 1 | 25 | F |
| **F** | 0 | 10 | A | 1 | 10 | A | 1 | 10 | A |
| **G** | 0 | ∞ | 0 | 0 | ∞ | 0 | 0 | 24 | E |

|        | D |  |  | C |  |  | B |  |  |
|--------|-------|-----|-----|-------|-----|-----|-------|-----|-----|
| Vertex | Known | dv | pv | Known | dv | pv | Known | dv | pv |
| **A** | 1 | 0 | 0 | 1 | 0 | 0 | 1 | 0 | 0 |
| **B** | 0 | 28 | A | 0 | 16 | C | 1 | 16 | C |
| **C** | 0 | 12 | D | 1 | 12 | D | 1 | 12 | D |
| **D** | 1 | 22 | E | 1 | 22 | E | 1 | 22 | E |
| **E** | 1 | 25 | F | 1 | 25 | F | 1 | 25 | F |
| **F** | 1 | 10 | A | 1 | 10 | A | 1 | 10 | A |
| **G** | 0 | 24 | E | 0 | 24 | E | 0 | 14 | B |

| | G | | |
|---|---|---|---|
| Vertex | Known | dv | pv |
| A | 1 | 0 | 0 |
| B | 1 | 16 | C |
| C | 1 | 12 | D |
| D | 1 | 22 | E |
| E | 1 | 25 | F |
| F | 1 | 10 | A |
| G | 1 | 14 | B |

## *Program to Implement Prims Algorithm*

```c
#include<stdio.h>
#include<conio.h>
int a,b,u,v,n,i,j,ne=1;
int visited[10]={0},min,mincost=0,cost[10][10];
void main()
{
printf("\n Enter the number of nodes:");
scanf("%d",&n);
printf("\n Enter the adjacency matrix:\n");
for(i=1;i<=n;i++)
for(j=1;j<=n;j++)
{
scanf("%d",&cost[i][j]);
if(cost[i][j]==0)
cost[i][j]=999;
}
visited[1]=1;
printf("\n");
while(ne<n)
{
for(i=1,min=999;i<=n;i++)
for(j=1;j<=n;j++)
```

```
if(cost[i][j]<min)
if(visited[i]!=0)
{
    min=cost[i][j];
     a=u=i;
      b=v=j;
}
 if(visited[u]==0 || visited[v]==0)
 {
 printf("\n Edge %d:(%d %d) cost:%d",ne++,a,b,min);
 mincost+=min;
 visited[b]=1;
 }
 cost[a][b]=cost[b][a]=999;
 }
 printf("\n Minimun cost=%d",mincost);
 }
```

### 7.6.2. *Kruskal's Algorithm*

A minimum spanning tree (MST) or minimum weight spanning tree for a weighted, connected and undirected graph is a spanning tree with weight less than or equal to the weight of every other spanning tree. The weight of a spanning tree is the sum of weights given to each edge of the spanning tree. A minimum spanning tree has (V – 1) edges where V is the number of vertices in the given graph.

### *Steps for Finding MST Using Kruskal's Algorithm*

i.      Sort all the edges in non-decreasing order of their weight.

ii.     Pick the smallest edge. Check if it forms a cycle with the spanning tree formed so far. If cycle is not formed, include this edge. Else, discard it.

iii.    Repeat step#2 until there are (V-1) edges in the spanning tree.

The algorithm is a Greedy Algorithm. The Greedy Choice is to pick the smallest weight edge that does not cause a cycle in the MST constructed so far.

# Example 1

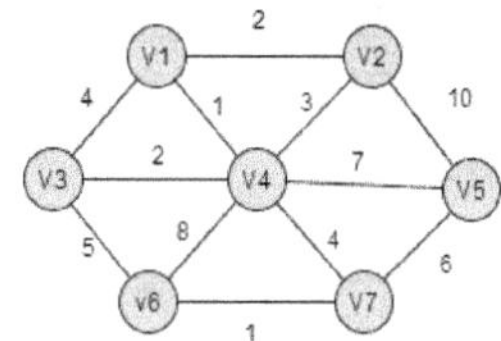

| Edge | Weight | Action |
|------|--------|--------|
| (v1, v4) | 1 | Accepted |
| (v6, v7) | 1 | Accepted |
| (v1, v2) | 2 | Accepted |
| (v3, v4) | 2 | Accepted |
| (v2, v4) | 3 | Rejected |
| (v1, v3) | 4 | Rejected |
| (v4, v7) | 4 | Accepted |
| (v3, v6) | 5 | Rejected |
| (v5, v7) | 6 | Accepted |

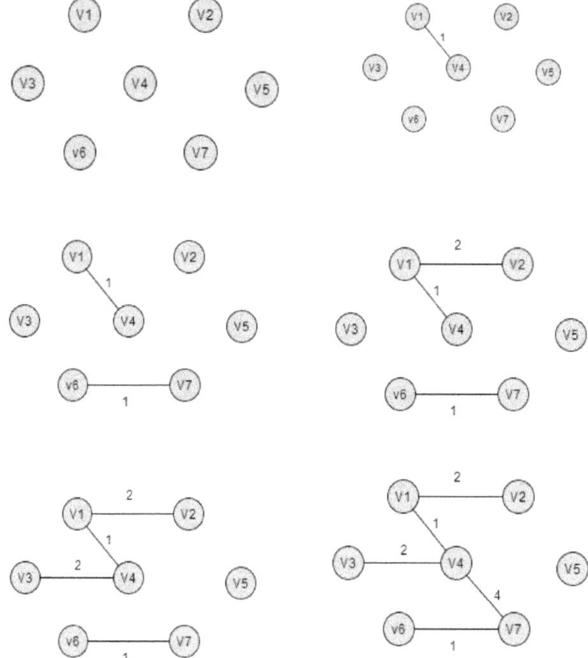

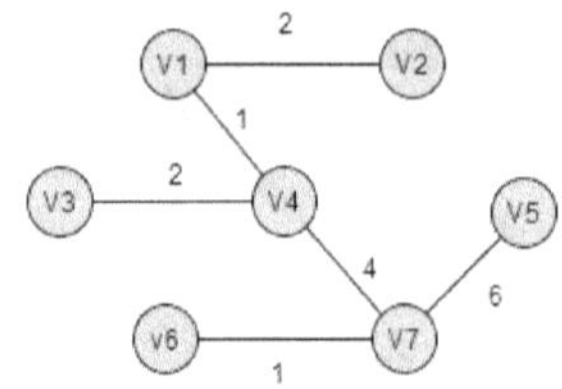

## Example 2

Consider the below input graph.

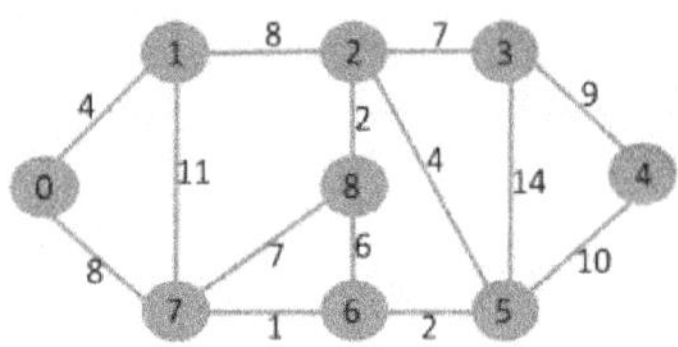

The graph contains 9 vertices and 14 edges. So, the minimum spanning tree formed will be having (9 – 1) = 8 edges.

After Sorting:

| Edge | Weight | Action |
|---|---|---|
| (v7, v6) | 1 | Accepted |
| (v8, v2) | 2 | Accepted |
| (v6, v5) | 2 | Accepted |
| (v0, v1) | 4 | Accepted |
| (v2, v5) | 4 | Accepted |
| (v8, v6) | 6 | Rejected |
| (v2, v3) | 7 | Accepted |
| (v7, v8) | 7 | Rejected |
| (v0, v7) | 8 | Accepted |
| (v1, v2) | 8 | Rejected |
| (v3, v4) | 9 | Accepted |
| (v5, v4) | 10 | Rejected |
| (v1, v7) | 11 | Rejected |
| (v3, v5) | 14 | Rejected |

Now pick all edges one by one from sorted list of edges

1. Pick edge 7-6: No cycle is formed, include it.

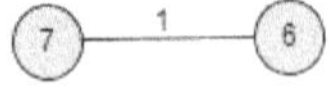

2.   Pick edge 8-2: No cycle is formed, include it.

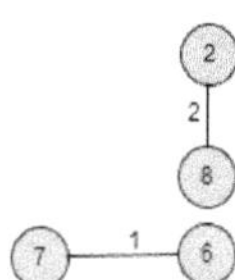

3.   Pick edge 6-5: No cycle is formed, include it.

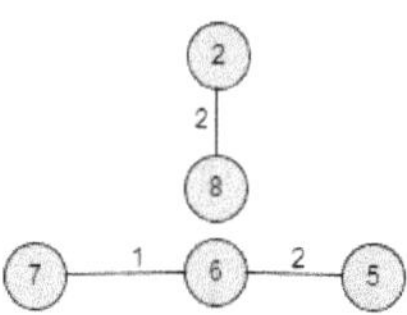

4.   Pick edge 0-1: No cycle is formed, include it.

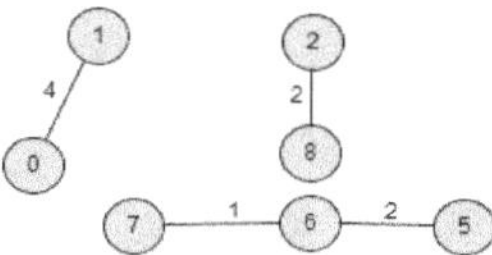

5.   *Pick edge 2-5:* No cycle is formed, include it.

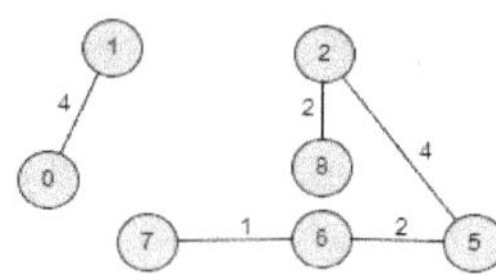

6.   Pick edge 8-6:Since including this edge results in cycle, discard it.

7.   Pick edge 2-3: No cycle is formed, include it.

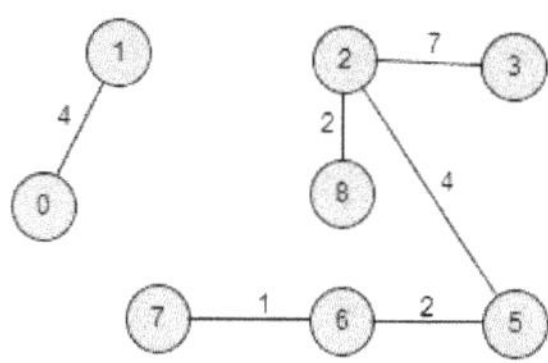

8.   Pick edge 7-8: Since including this edge results in cycle, discard it.

9.   Pick edge 0-7: No cycle is formed, include it.

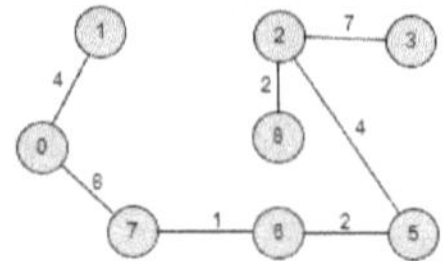

10. Pick edge 1-2:Since including this edge results in cycle, discard it.

11. Pick edge 3-4: No cycle is formed, include it.

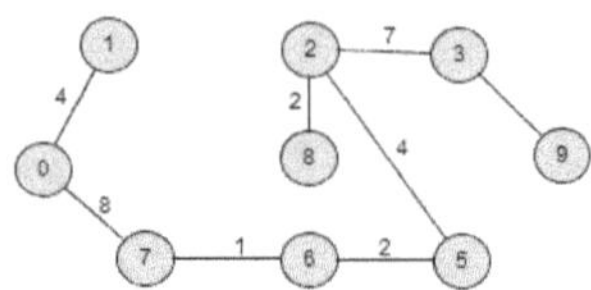

Since the number of edges included equals (V – 1), the algorithm stops here.

### *Routine*

```
Void Kruskal(Graph G)
{
int EdgesAccepted;
DijiSet S;
PriorityQueue H;
Vertex U,V;
SetType Uset,Vset;
Edge E;
Initialize(S);
ReadGraphIntoHeapArray(G,H);
BuildHeap(H);
EdgesAccepted=0;
While(EdgesAccepted<NumVertex-1)
{
E=DeleteMin(H);
Uset=Find(U,S);
Vset=Find(V,S);
If(Uset!=Vset)
{
EdgesAccepted++;
SetUnion(S, Uset, Vset);
}}
}
```

## 7.7.    Graph Traversal

Traversing graph is the efficient way to visit each vertex and edge exactly once.

A traversal (search):

- An algorithm for systematically exploring a graph
- Visiting (all) vertices
- Until finding a goal vertex or until no more vertices

Only for connected graphs

### *Types*

Breadth-first search (BFS)

Depth-first search (DFS)

### *7.7.1.  Breadth-first Search (BFS)*

Breadth-first search (BFS) is an algorithm for traversing or searching tree or graph data structures. It starts at the tree root (or some arbitrary node of a graph, sometimes referred to as a 'search key') and explores the neighbour nodes first, before moving to the next level neighbours.

Breadth First Search (BFS) algorithm traverses a graph in a breadth ward motion and uses a queue to remember to get the next vertex to start a search, when a dead end occurs in any iteration.

**Rule 1** – Visit the adjacent unvisited vertex. Mark, it as visited. Display it. Insert it in a queue.

**Rule 2** – If no adjacent vertex is found, remove the first vertex from the queue.

**Rule 3** – Repeat Rule 1 and Rule 2 until the queue is empty.

### *Algorithm*

**Step 1**: Push the root node in the Queue.

**Step 2**: Loop until the queue is empty.

**Step 3**:Remove the node from the Queue.

**Step 4**: If the removed node has unvisited child nodes, mark them as visited and insert the unvisited children in the queue

## *Example*

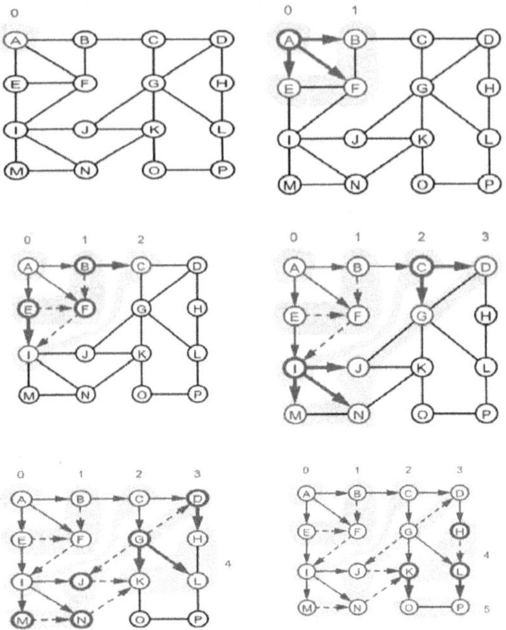

## *Example*

| Step | Traversal | Description |
| --- | --- | --- |
| 1 | 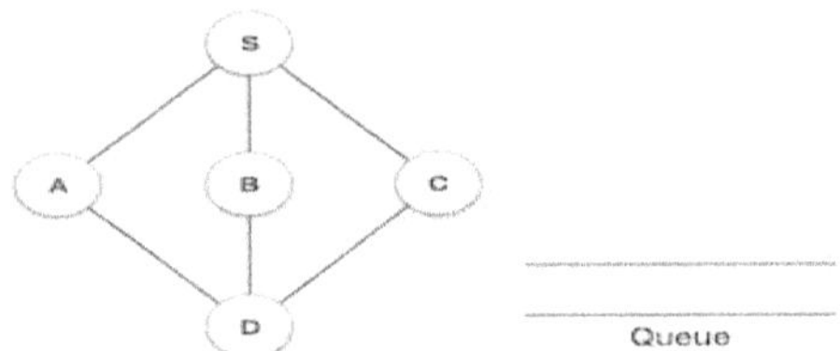 | Initialize the queue. |

| 2 | 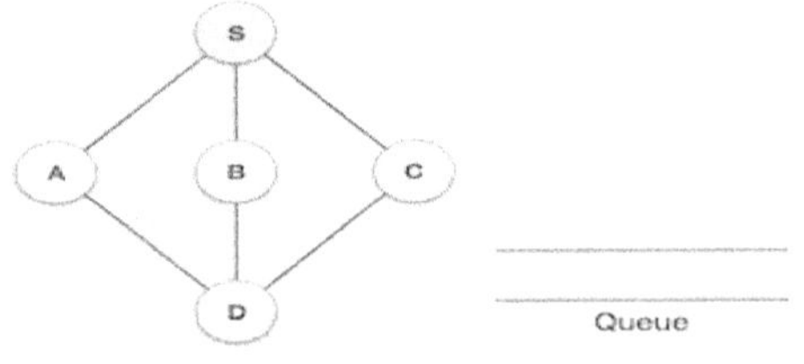 | We start from visiting **S** (starting node), and mark it as visited. |

3

We then see an unvisited adjacent node from S. In this example, we have three nodes but alphabetically we choose A, mark it as visited and enqueue it.

4

Next, the unvisited adjacent node from S is B. We mark it as visited and enqueue it.

5

Next, the unvisited adjacent node from S is C. We mark it as visited and enqueue it.

6

Now, S is left with no unvisited adjacent nodes. So, we dequeue and find A.

7

From A we have D as unvisited adjacent node. We mark it as visited and enqueue it.

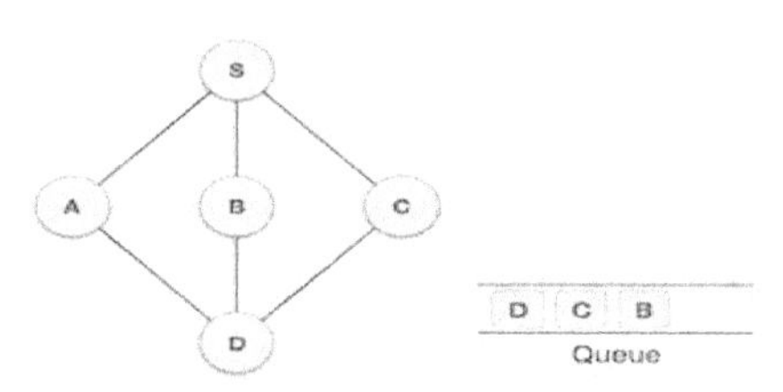

Solution: S A B C D

## *Program for BFS*

```c
#include<stdio.h>
#include<conio.h>
int a[20][20],q[20],visited[20],n,i,j,f=0,r=-1;
void bfs(int v)
{
 for(i=1;i<=n;i++)
  if(a[v][i] && !visited[i])
   q[++r]=i;
 if(f<=r)
 {
  visited[q[f]]=1;
  bfs(q[f++]);
 }
}
void main()
{
 int v;
 clrscr();
 printf("\n Enter the number of vertices:");
 scanf("%d",&n);
 for(i=1;i<=n;i++)
 {
  q[i]=0;
  visited[i]=0;
 }
 printf("\n Enter graph data in matrix form:\n");
 for(i=1;i<=n;i++)
  for(j=1;j<=n;j++)
   scanf("%d",&a[i][j]);
 printf("\n Enter the starting vertex:");
 scanf("%d",&v);
 bfs(v);
 printf("\n The node which are reachable are:\n");
```

```
for(i=1;i<=n;i++)
 if(visited[i])
  printf("%d\t",i);
 else
  printf("\n Bfs is not possible");
 getch();
 }
```

### 7.7.2. *Depth First Search (DFS)*

Depth First Search (DFS) algorithm traverses a graph in a depthward motion and uses a stack to remember to get the next vertex to start a search, when a dead end occurs in any iteration.

- **Rule 1** – Visit the adjacent unvisited vertex. Mark, it as visited. Display it. Push it in a stack.
- **Rule 2** – If no adjacent vertex is found, pop up a vertex from the stack. (It will pop up all the vertices from the stack, which do not have adjacent vertices.)
- **Rule 3** – Repeat Rule 1 and Rule 2 until the stack is empty.

### *Example*

| Step | Traversal | Description |
|------|-----------|-------------|
| 1 | 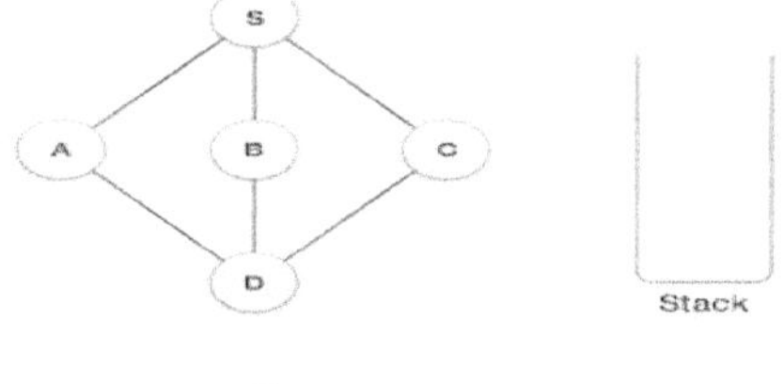 | Initialize the stack. |
| 2 | 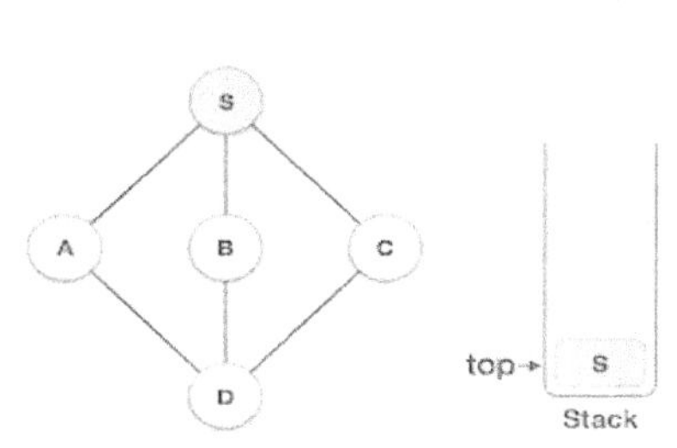 | Mark S as visited and put it onto the stack. Explore any unvisited adjacent node from **S**. We have three nodes and we can pick any of them. For this example, we shall take the node in an alphabetical order. |

3

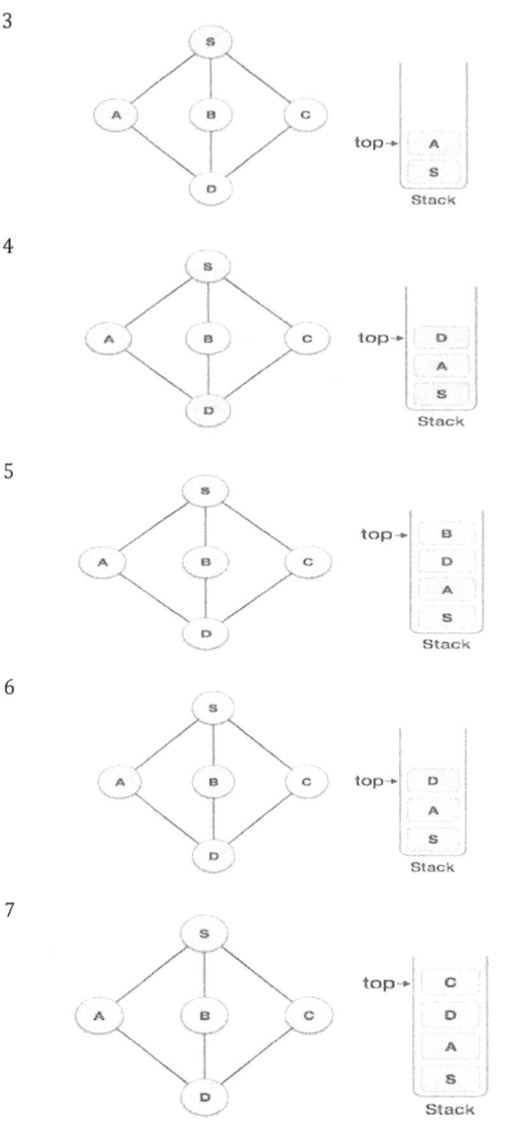

Mark A as visited and put it onto the stack. Explore any unvisited adjacent node from A. Both **S** and D are adjacent to A but we are concerned for unvisited nodes only.

4

Visit D and mark it as visited and put onto the stack. Here, we have B and C nodes, which are adjacent to D and both are unvisited. However, we shall again choose in an alphabetical order.

5

We choose B, mark it as visited and put onto the stack. Here B does not have any unvisited adjacent node. So, we pop B from the stack.

6

We check the stack top for return to the previous node and check if it has any unvisited nodes. Here, we find D to be on the top of the stack.

7

Only unvisited adjacent node is from Dis Cnow. So we visit C, mark it as visited and put it onto the stack.

Solution: S A D B C

As **C** does not have any unvisited adjacent node so we keep popping the stack until we find a node that has an unvisited adjacent node. In this case, there's none and we keep popping until the stack is empty.

## *Program for DFS*

```c
#include<stdio.h>
#include<conio.h>
int a[20][20],reach[20],n;
void dfs(int v)
{
 int i;
 reach[v]=1;
 for(i=1;i<=n;i++)
  if(a[v][i] && !reach[i])
  {
   printf("\n %d->%d",v,i);
   dfs(i);
  }
}
void main()
{
 int i,j,count=0;
 clrscr();
 printf("\n Enter number of vertices:");
 scanf("%d",&n);
 for(i=1;i<=n;i++)
 {
  reach[i]=0;
  for(j=1;j<=n;j++)
   a[i][j]=0;
 }
 printf("\n Enter the adjacency matrix:\n");
 for(i=1;i<=n;i++)
  for(j=1;j<=n;j++)
   scanf("%d",&a[i][j]);
 dfs(1);
 printf("\n");
 for(i=1;i<=n;i++)
```

```
    {
    if(reach[i])
    count++;
    }
    if(count==n)
    printf("\n Graph is connected");
    else
    printf("\n Graph is not connected");
    getch();
```

## 7.8.  Application of DFS

### 1.  *Bi-Connectivity*

A connected undirected graph is biconnected if there are no vertices whose removal disconnects the rest of the graph.

Example:

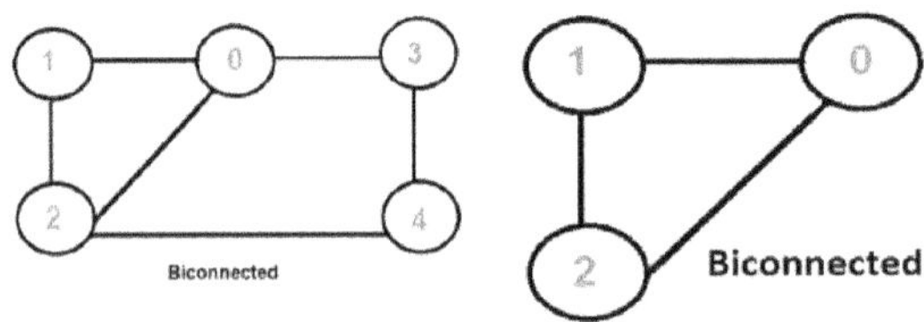


### 2.  *Articulation Point*

A vertex in an undirected connected graph is an articulation point (or cut vertex) if removing it (and edges through it) disconnects the graph. i.e., The vertices whose removal would disconnects the graph.

Example:

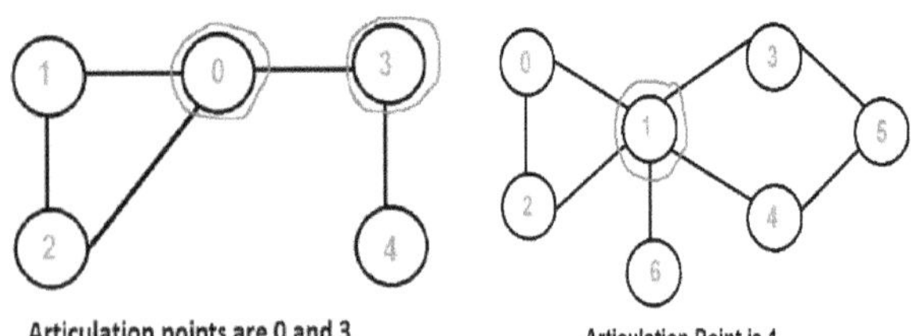

## *Example*

DFS with Num and Low

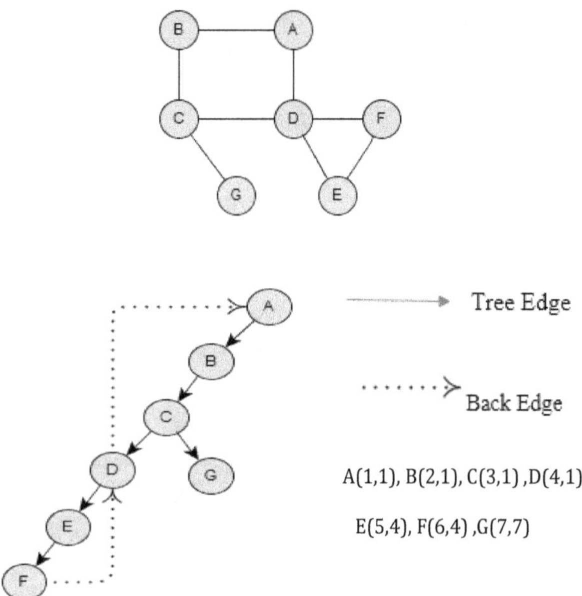



a. Find Post-Order Traversal.

F E D G C B A

b. Find Num(V)

Num(A)=1, Num(B)=2, Num(C)=3, Num(D)=4,Num(E)=5, Nunm(F)=4, Num(G)=7

c. Find Low(V)

(i) Back edge- Num(V)

(ii) Tree edge-Low(V)

1. Low(F)=Min(Num(F),Num(D))  = (6,4) = 4

   Low(F)= 4

2. Low(E)=Min(Num(E), Low(F))  =(5,4)=4

   Low(E)=4

3. Low(D)=Min(Num(D),Low(E),Num(A))  =Min(4,4,1)= 1

Low(D)= 1

4. Low(G)=Min(Num(G))

   Low(G)=7

5. Low(C)=Min(Num(C),Low(D),Low(G))          =Min(3,1,7)

   Low(C)= 1

6. Low(B)=Min(Num(B),Low(G))

   Low(B) =Min(2,1)=1

7. Low(A)=Min(Num(A),Low(B))

   Low(A) =Min(1,1) = 1

# CHAPTER 8

# SORTING

Sorting refers to arranging data in a particular format. Sorting algorithm specifies the way to arrange data in a particular order. Most common orders are in numerical or lexicographical order.

## 8.1.  Types of Sorting

If the number of objects is small enough to fits into the main memory, sorting is called internal sorting.

### *Example*

- Bucket sort
- Bubble sort
- Insertion sort
- Selection sort
- Heap sort
- Merge sort

If the number of objects is so large that some of them reside on external storage during the sort, it is called external sorting.

The importance of sorting lies in the fact that data searching can be optimized to a very high level, if data is stored in a sorted manner. Sorting is also used to represent data in more readable formats. Following are some of the examples of sorting in real-life scenarios

**Telephone Directory**–The telephone directory stores the telephone numbers of people sorted by their names, so that the names can be searched easily.

**Dictionary**–The dictionary stores words in an alphabetical order so that searching of any word becomes easy.

### *In-place Sorting and Not-in-place Sorting*

- Sorting algorithms may require some extra space for comparison and temporary storage of few data elements. These algorithms do not require any extra space and sorting is said to happen in-place, or for example, within the array itself. This is called **in-place sorting**. Bubble sort is an example of in-place sorting.

- However, in some sorting algorithms, the program requires space which is more than or equal to the elements being sorted. Sorting which uses equal or more space is called **not-in-place sorting**. Merge-sort is an example of not-in-place sorting.

### Stable and Not Stable Sorting

If a sorting algorithm, after sorting the contents, does not change the sequence of similar content in which they appear, it is called stable sorting.

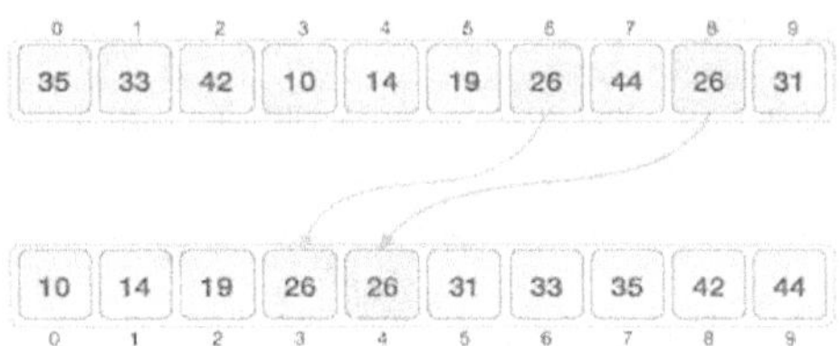

If a sorting algorithm, after sorting the contents, changes the sequence of similar content in which they appear, it is called unstable sorting.

Stability of an algorithm matters when we wish to maintain the sequence of original elements, like in a tuple for example.

### Adaptive and Non-Adaptive Sorting Algorithm

A sorting algorithm is said to be adaptive, if it takes advantage of already 'sorted' elements in the list that is to be sorted. That is, while sorting if the source list has some element already sorted, adaptive algorithms will take this into account and will try not to re-order them.

A non-adaptive algorithm is one which does not take into account the elements which are already sorted. They try to force every single element to be re-ordered to confirm their sortedness.

### Important Terms

Some terms are generally coined while discussing sorting techniques, here is a brief introduction to them

### *Increasing Order*

A sequence of values is said to be in increasing order, if the successive element is greater than the previous one. For example, 1, 3, 4, 6, 8, 9 are in increasing order, as every next element is greater than the previous element.

### *Decreasing Order*

A sequence of values is said to be in decreasing order, if the successive element is less than the current one. For example, 9, 8, 6, 4, 3, 1 are in decreasing order, as every next element is less than the previous element.

### *Non-Increasing Order*

A sequence of values is said to be in non-increasing order, if the successive element is less than or equal to its previous element in the sequence. This order occurs when the sequence contains duplicate values. For example, 9, 8, 6, 3, 3, 1 are in non-increasing order, as every next element is less than or equal to (in case of 3) but not greater than any previous element.

### *Non-Decreasing Order*

A sequence of values is said to be in non-decreasing order, if the successive element is greater than or equal to its previous element in the sequence. This order occurs when the sequence contains duplicate values. For example, 1, 3, 3, 6, 8, 9 are in non-decreasing order, as every next element is greater than or equal to (in case of 3) but not less than the previous one.

## 8.2.  Insertion Sort

Insertion sort is a simple sorting algorithm that works the way we sort playing cards in our hands. The array is searched sequentially and unsorted items are moved and inserted into the sorted sub-list (in the same array). This algorithm is not suitable for large data sets as its average and worst case complexity are of $O(n^2)$, where **n** is the number of items.

### *Algorithm*

**Step 1** – If it is the first element, it is already sorted. return 1;

Step 2 – Pick next element

**Step 3** – Compare with all elements in the sorted sub-list

**Step 4** – Shift all the elements in the sorted sub-list that is greater than    the value to be sorted

**Step 5** – Insert the value

**Step 6**– Repeat until list is sorted

## *Example 1*

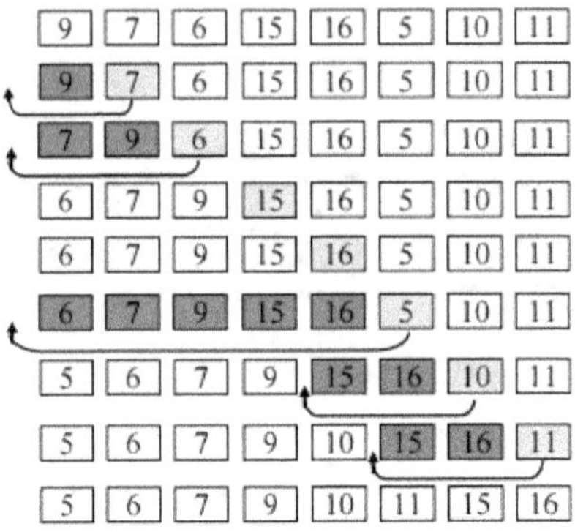

## *Example 2*

We take an unsorted array for our example.

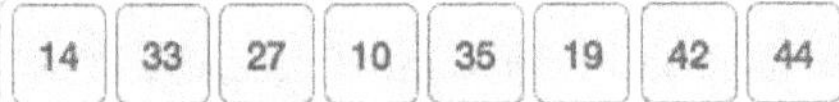

Insertion sort compares the first two elements.

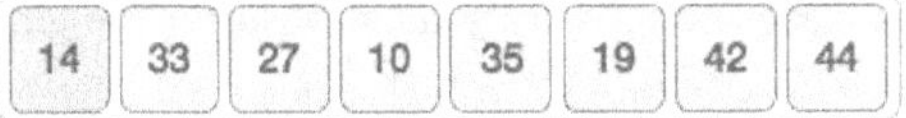

It finds that both 14 and 33 are already in ascending order. For now, 14 is in sorted sub-list.

Insertion sort moves ahead and compares 33 with 27.

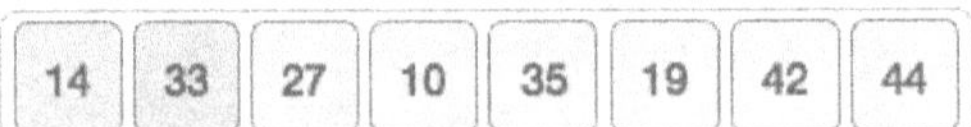

And finds that 33 is not in the correct position.

It swaps 33 with 27. It also checks with all the elements of sorted sub-list. Here we see that the sorted sub-list has only one element 14, and 27 is greater than 14. Hence, the sorted sub-list remains sorted after swapping.

By now we have 14 and 27 in the sorted sub-list. Next, it compares 33 with 10.

These values are not in a sorted order.

So, we swap them.

However, swapping makes 27 and 10 unsorted.

Hence, we swap them too.

Again, we find 14 and 10 in an unsorted order.

We swap them again. By the end of third iteration, we have a sorted sub-list of 4 items.

This process goes on until all the unsorted values are covered in a sorted sub-list.

## *Example 3*

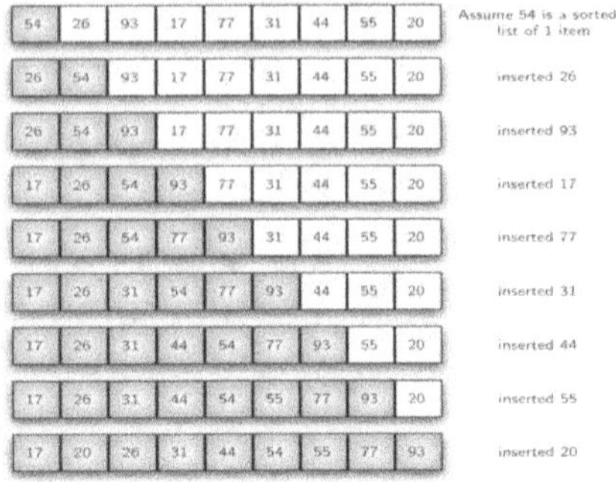

## *Program for Insertion Sort*

```c
#include<stdio.h>
int main(){
 int i,j,s,temp,a[20];
 printf("Enter total elements: ");
 scanf("%d",&s);
 printf("Enter %d elements: ",s);
 for(i=0;i<s;i++)
   scanf("%d",&a[i]);
 for(i=1;i<s;i++){
   temp=a[i];
   j=i-1;
   while((temp<a[j])&&(j>=0)){
   a[j+1]=a[j];
     j=j-1;
   }
   a[j+1]=temp;
 }
 printf("After sorting: ");
 for(i=0;i<s;i++)
   printf(" %d",a[i]);
 return 0;
}
```

## 8.3.    Shell Sort

Shell sort is a sorting algorithm, devised by Donald Shell in 1959. Shell sort is a highly efficient sorting algorithm and is based on insertion sort algorithm. This algorithm avoids large shifts as in case of insertion sort, if the smaller value is to the far right and has to be moved to the far left. It is also called as Diminishing Increment shell.

### *Steps*

1.   K=N/2, where N is the number of elements in the array
2.   K=K/2

### *Example 1*

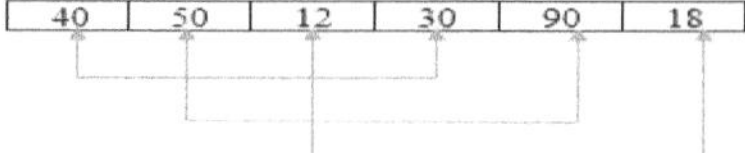

| 40 | 50 | 12 | 30 | 90 | 18 |

N=6; K=N/2=3

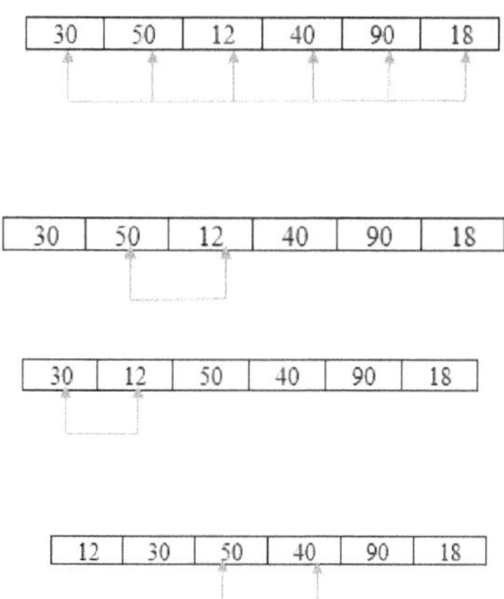

K=3/2=1

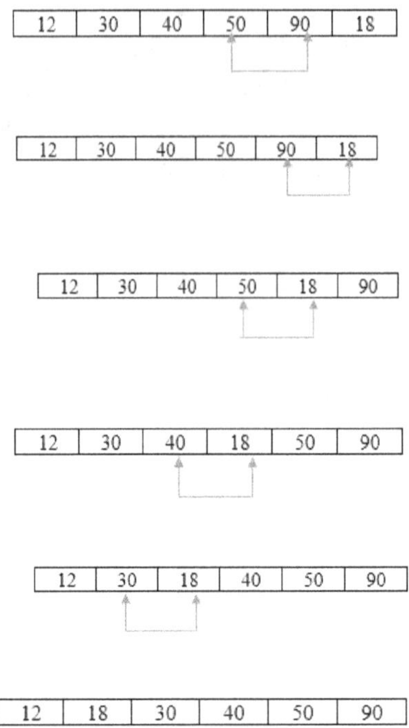

## Program for Shell Sort

```c
#include<stdio.h>
#include<conio.h>
int main()
{
int arr[30];
int i,j,k,tmp,num;
printf("Enter total no. of elements : ");
scanf("%d", &num);
for(k=0; k<num; k++)
{
 printf("\nEnter %d number : ",k+1);
 scanf("%d",&arr[k]);
}
```

```c
for(i=num/2; i>0; i=i/2)
{
  for(j=i; j<num; j++)
  {
    for(k=j-i; k>=0; k=k-i)
    {
      if(arr[k+i]>=arr[k])
        break;
      else
      {
        tmp=arr[k];
        arr[k]=arr[k+i];
        arr[k+i]=tmp;
      }
    }
  }
}
printf("\t**** Shell Sorting ****\n");
for(k=0; k<num; k++)
  printf("%d\t",arr[k]);
getch();
return 0;
}
```

## 8.4.    Heap Sort

Heap sort is a comparison based sorting technique based on Binary Heap data structure. It is similar to selection sort where we first find the maximum element and place the maximum element at the end (Max Heap).

We repeat the same process for remaining element. Heap sort algorithm is divided into two basic parts:

- Creating a Heap of the unsorted list.
- Then a sorted array is created by repeatedly removing the largest/smallest element from the heap, and inserting it into the array. The heap is reconstructed after each removal.

### *What is a Heap?*

Heap is a special tree-based data structure, that satisfies the following special heap properties:

1. **Structure Property:** Heap data structure is always a Complete Binary Tree, which means all levels of the tree are fully filled.

2. **Heap Property:** All nodes are either [greater than or equal to] or [less than or equal to] each of its children. If the parent nodes are greater than their children, heap is called a Max-Heap, and if the parent nodes are smaller than their child nodes, heap is called Min-Heap.

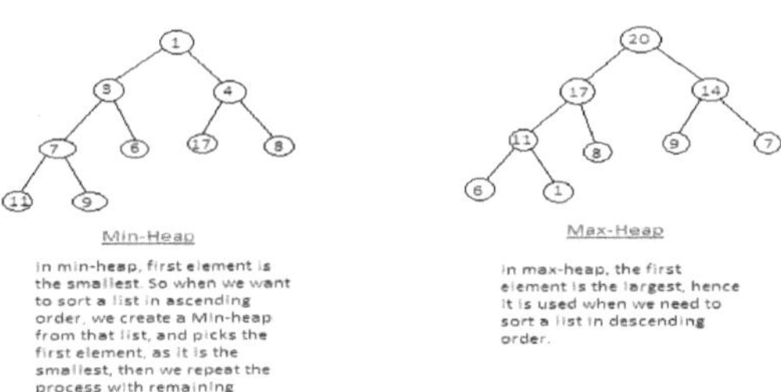



A= {5,13,2,25,7,17,20,8,4}

Insert as structure property order

Swap 13 with 25 and 2 with 20

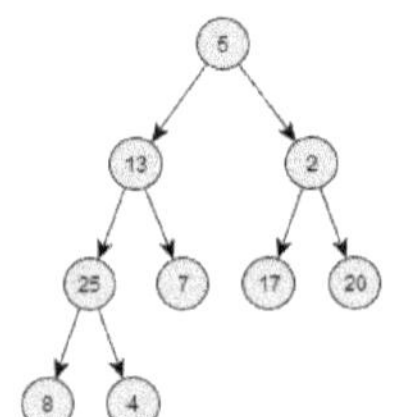

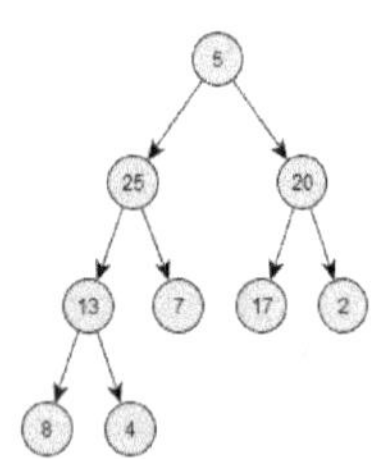

Swap 25 with 5 as greater number should be at the top in max heap

Swap 13 with 5

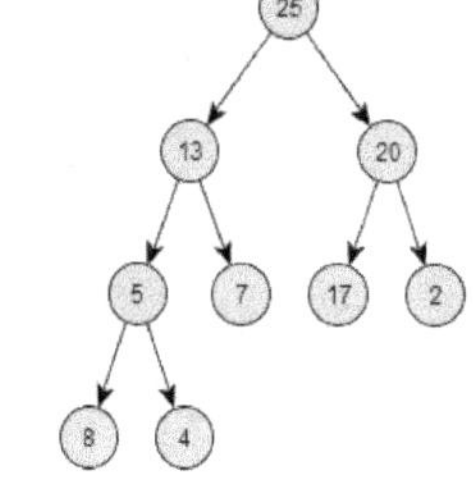

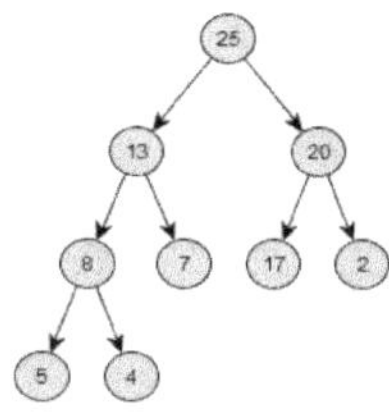

Finally, we build the maxheap tree as

## *Maxheap Deletion*

Swap last element 4 with topmost element 25 and remove 25 and check for maxheap condition.

Swap 20 with 4 (Max Heap)

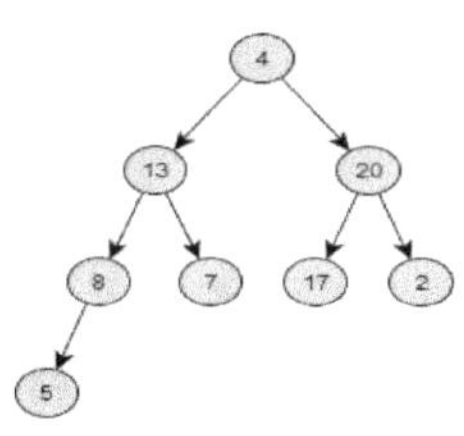

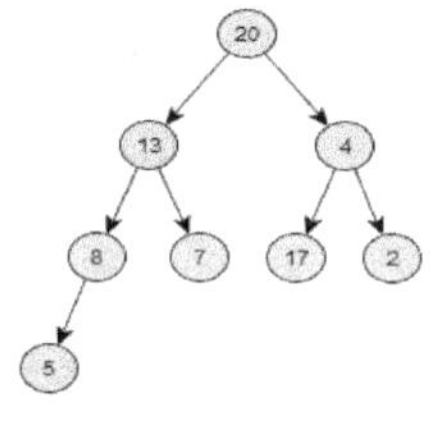

Swap maximum element 20 by the last element 5 and remove 20

Swap 17 with 5(Max Heap)

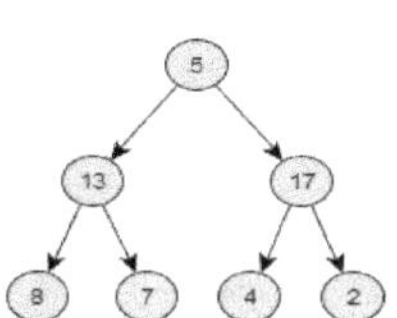

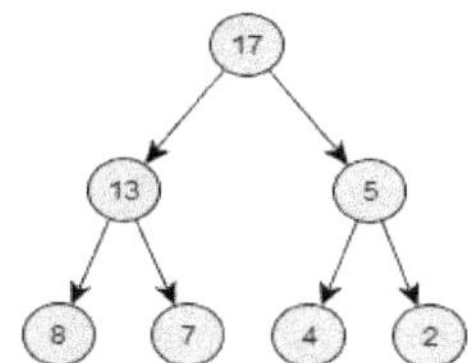

Swap last element 2 with maximum element 17 and remove 17    Swap 13 with 2 and 2 with 8 (Max Heap)

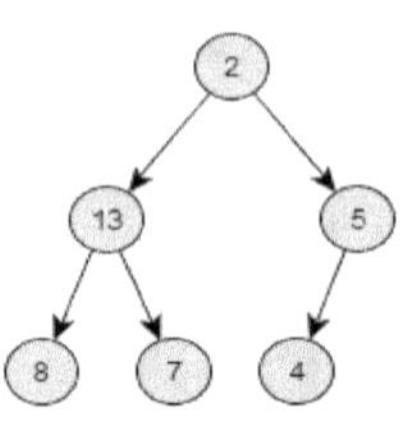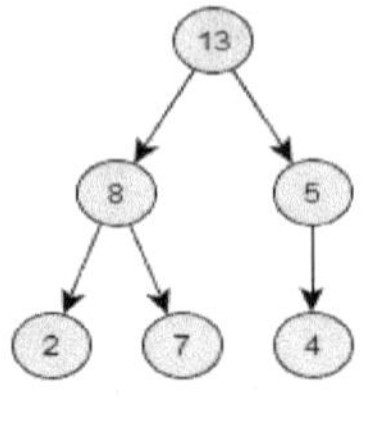

Swap last element 4 with maximum element 13 and remove 13    Swap 8 with 4

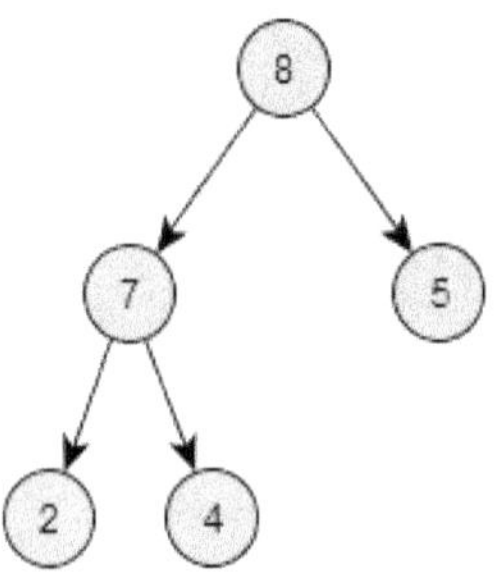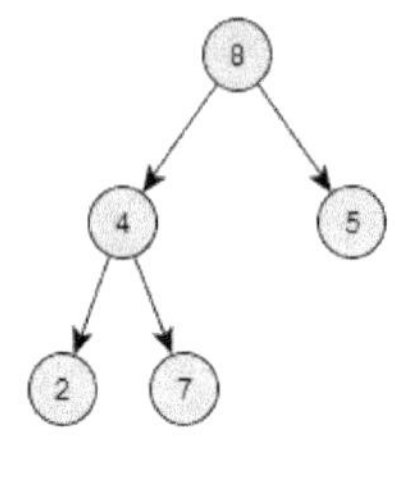

Swap 7 with 4 (Max Heap)    Swap last element 4 with maximum element 8 and remove 8

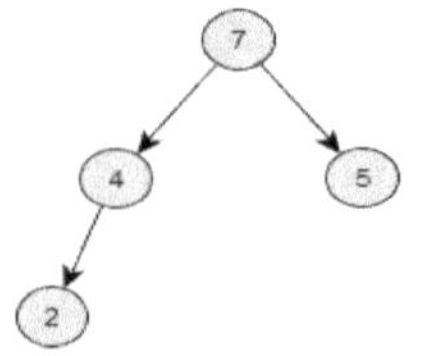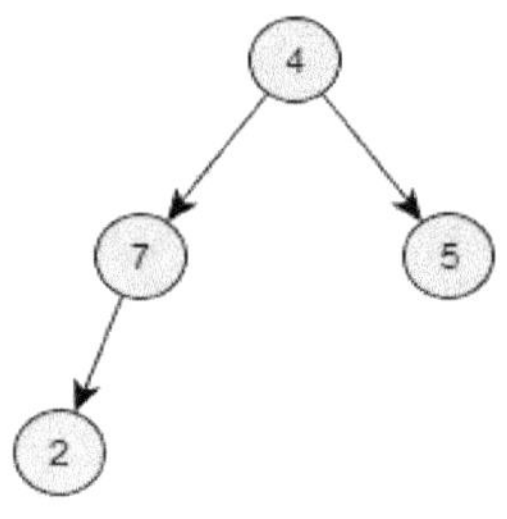

Swap 7 with 4 (Max Heap)    Swap last element 2 with maximum element 7 and remove 7

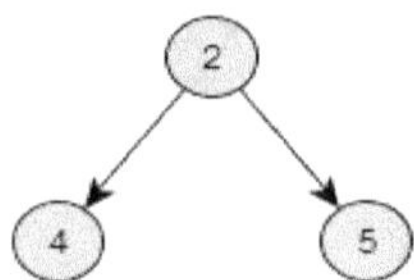

Swap 5 with 2 (Max Heap)

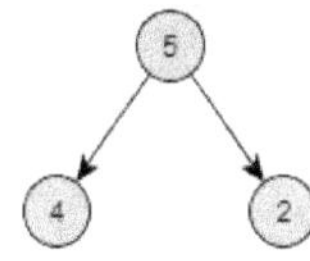

Swap 2 with 4 (Max Heap)

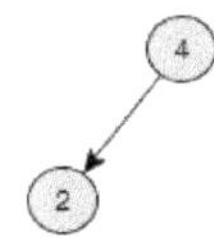

Swap last element 2 with maximum element 5 and remove 5

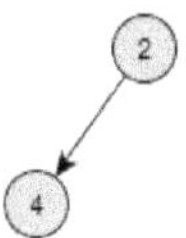

Swap last element 2 with maximum element 4 and remove 4

## *Program for Heap Sort*

```c
#include<stdio.h>
#include<conio.h>
int temp,ap;
void input(int *a,int n)
{
   int i;
   printf("Enter %d elements....\n",n);
   for(i=0;i<n;i++)
     scanf("%d",&a[i]);
}
void output(int *a,int n)
{
   int i;
   for(i=0;i<n;i++)
     printf("%d,",a[i]);
}void maxheap(int *a,int i,int n)
{
   int child,temp;
   for(temp=a[i];(2*i+1)<n;i=child)
   {
     child= 2*i+1;
     if((child!=n-1)&&(a[child+1]>a[child]))
       child++;
```

```c
        if(temp<a[child])
            a[i]=a[child];
        else
            break;
    }
    a[i]=temp;
}
void heapsort(int *a,int n)
{
    int i;
    for(i=n/2;i>=0;i--)
    {
        maxheap(a,i,n);
    }
    for(i=n-1;i>=0;i--)
    {
        int t;
        t=a[0];
        a[0]=a[i];
        a[i]=t;
        maxheap(a,0,i);
    }
}
int main()
{
    int a[25],n;
        printf("Enter the no of elements...");
        scanf("%d",&n);
        input(a,n);
        printf("\nThe elements in the array before sorting...");
        output(a,n);
        heapsort(a,n);
        printf("\nThe elements in the array after sorting...");
        output(a,n);
}
```

## 8.5.  Merge Sort

Merge sort is general-purpose, comparison-based sorting algorithm. Merge Sort is a Divide and Conquer algorithm. It divides input array in two halves, calls itself for the two halves and then merges the two sorted halves. The merge () function is used for merging two halves. The merge (arr, l, m, r) is key process that assumes that arr[l..m] and arr[m+1..r] are sorted and merges the two sorted sub-arrays into one.

### *Algorithm*

MergeSort(arr[], l,  r)

If r > l

1. Find the middle point to divide the array into two halves:

middle m = (l+r)/2

2. Call mergeSort for first half:

Call mergeSort(arr, l, m)

3. Call mergeSort for second half:

Call mergeSort(arr, m+1, r)

4. Merge the two halves sorted in step 2 and 3:

Call merge(arr, l, m, r)

### *Example 1*

A= {38, 27, 43, 3, 9, 82, 10}.

The array is recursively divided in two halves till the size becomes 1. Once the size becomes 1, the merge processes comes into action and starts merging arrays back till the complete array is merged.

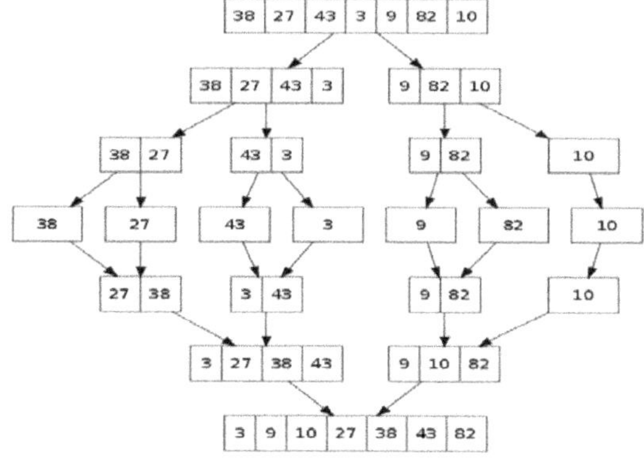

### *Program for Merge Sort*

```c
#include<stdlib.h>
#include<stdio.h>
// Merges two subarrays of arr[].
// First subarray is arr[l..m]
// Second subarray is arr[m+1..r]
void merge(int arr[], int l, int m, int r)
{
    int i, j, k;
    int n1 = m - l + 1;
    int n2 =  r - m;
    /* create temp arrays */
    int L[n1], R[n2];
    /* Copy data to temp arrays L[] and R[] */
    for (i = 0; i < n1; i++)
        L[i] = arr[l + i];
    for (j = 0; j < n2; j++)
        R[j] = arr[m + 1+ j];
    /* Merge the temp arrays back into arr[l..r]*/
    i = 0; // Initial index of first subarray
    j = 0; // Initial index of second subarray
    k = l; // Initial index of merged subarray
    while (i < n1 && j < n2)
    {
        if (L[i] <= R[j])
        {
            arr[k] = L[i];
            i++;
        }
        else
        {
            arr[k] = R[j];
            j++;
        }
```

```c
        k++;
    }
    /* Copy the remaining elements of L[], if there
       are any */
    while (i < n1)
    {
        arr[k] = L[i];
        i++;
        k++;
    }
    /* Copy the remaining elements of R[], if there
       are any */
    while (j < n2)
    {
        arr[k] = R[j];
        j++;
        k++;
    }
}
/* l is for left index and r is right index of the
   sub-array of arr to be sorted */
void mergeSort(int arr[], int l, int r)
{
    if (l < r)
    {
        // Same as (l+r)/2, but avoids overflow for
        // large l and h
        int m = l+(r-l)/2;
        // Sort first and second halves
        mergeSort(arr, l, m);
        mergeSort(arr, m+1, r);
        merge(arr, l, m, r);
    }
}
```

```c
/* UTILITY FUNCTIONS */
/* Function to print an array */
void printArray(int A[], int size)
{
   int i;
   for (i=0; i < size; i++)
      printf("%d ", A[i]);
   printf("\n");
}
/* Driver program to test above functions */
int main()
{
   int arr[] = {12, 11, 13, 5, 6, 7};
   int arr_size = sizeof(arr)/sizeof(arr[0]);
   printf("Given array is \n");
   printArray(arr, arr_size);
   mergeSort(arr, 0, arr_size - 1);
   printf("\nSorted array is \n");
   printArray(arr, arr_size);
   return 0;
}
```

## 8.6.  Quick Sort

The quick sort uses divide and conquer to gain the same advantages as the merge sort, while not using additional storage.

Quicksort is a very efficient sorting algorithm invented by C.A.R. Hoare. It has two phases:

- the partition phase and
- the sort phase.

In quicksort, we divide the array of items to be sorted into two partitions and then call the quicksort procedure recursively to sort the two partitions, i.e. we divide the problem into two smaller ones and conquer by solving the smaller ones

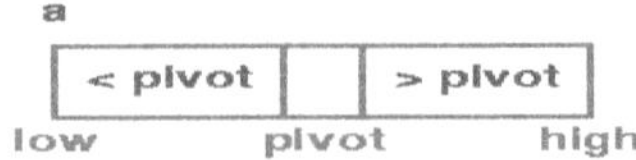

Initial step: Partition data

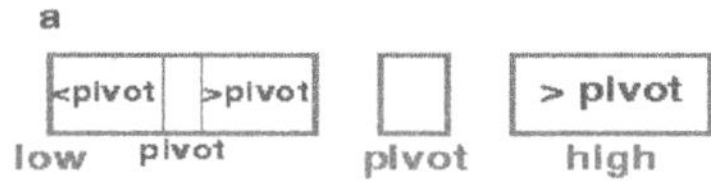


Sort Left partition in the same way

## *Algorithm*

Step 1: Choose first element as pivot, i and last element as j.

Step 2: Check for the condition

i<=p and i< l

j>p

Step 3: If i and j condition stops, swap the element of i and j.

Step 4: If i and j cross each other and if i and j at same place then swap the value of j and pivot element. The pivot element is placed in its correct position

Step 5: The quick sort procedure is applied for left and right array in recursive manner.

## *Program for Quick Sort*

```c
#include<stdio.h>
void quicksort(int [10],int,int);
int main()
{
 int x[20],size,i;
 printf("Enter size of the array: ");
 scanf("%d",&size);
 printf("Enter %d elements: ",size);
 for(i=0;i<size;i++)
  scanf("%d",&x[i]);
 quicksort(x,0,size-1);
 printf("Sorted elements: ");
 for(i=0;i<size;i++)
  printf(" %d",x[i]);
 return 0;
}
```

```c
void quicksort(int x[10],int first,int last){
   int pivot,j,temp,i;
   if(first<last){
      pivot=first;
      i=first;
      j=last;
      while(i<j){
         while(x[i]<=x[pivot]&&i<last)
            i++;
         while(x[j]>x[pivot])
            j--;
         if(i<j){
            temp=x[i];
            x[i]=x[j];
            x[j]=temp;
         }
      }
      temp=x[pivot];
      x[pivot]=x[j];
      x[j]=temp;
      quicksort(x,first,j-1);
      quicksort(x,j+1,last);
   }
}
```

## Example 1

We take an unsorted array for an example {40,20,70,14,60,61,97,30}

## Step 1

Choose first element (i) and pivot(p) as 40 and 30 as last element (j)

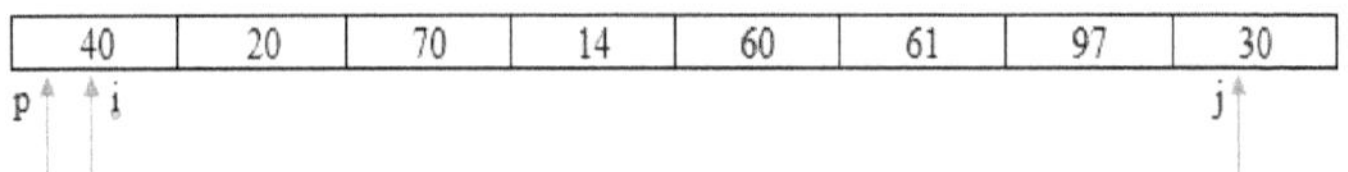

## Step 2

(i)check the condition i<=p

40<=40, Condition true so i pointer moves to the place of 20

20<=40, condition true so i pointer moves to 70

70<=40, condition false so i stops at 70

(ii) check for condition j>p

30>40 condition fails, so j pointer stops at 30 itself.

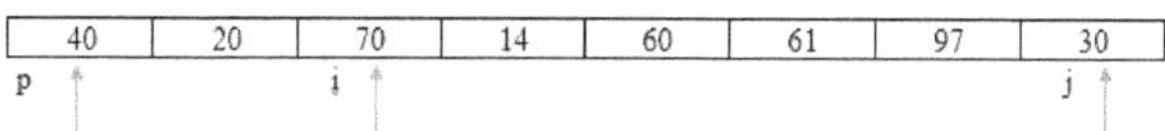

## Step 3

If i and j condition stops, swap the element of i and j

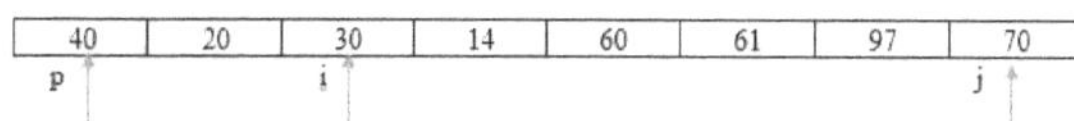

## Step 4

check for condition i<=p and j>p

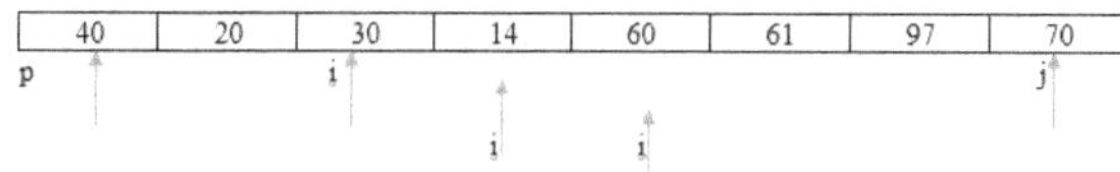

i pointer stops at 60 because i<=p condition fails (60<=40)

Next check for the condition j>p

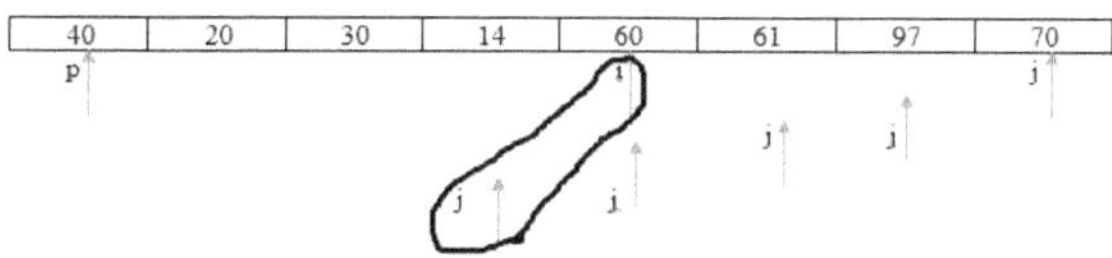

Here i pointer and j pointer crosses each other

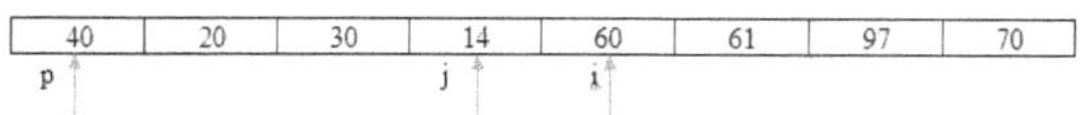

so, swap the value of j and pivot element

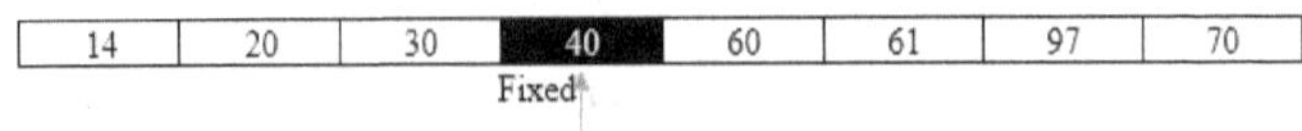

Once a value is fixed, the quick sort procedure is applied for left and right array in recursive manner.

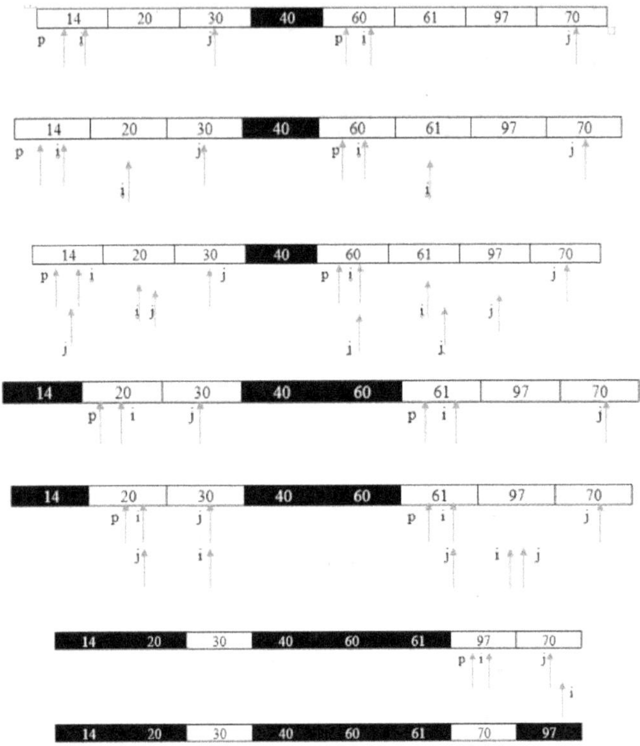

## 8.7.  Selection Sort

Selection sorting is conceptually the simplest sorting algorithm. This algorithm first finds the smallest element in the array and exchanges it with the element in the first position, then find the second smallest element and exchange it with the element in the second position, and continues in this way until the entire array is sorted.

This algorithm is not suitable for large data sets as its average and worst case complexities are of $O(n^2)$, where **n** is the number of items.

### Algorithm

**Step 1** – Set MIN to location 0

**Step 2** – Search the minimum element in the list

**Step 3** – Swap with value at location MIN

**Step 4** – Increment MIN to point to next element

**Step 5** – Repeat until list is sorted

### Example 1

Consider the following depicted array as an example.

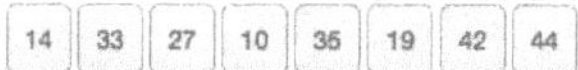

For the first position in the sorted list, the whole list is scanned sequentially. The first position where 14 is stored presently, we search the whole list and find that 10 is the lowest value.

So, we replace 14 with 10. After one iteration 10, which happens to be the minimum value in the list, appears in the first position of the sorted list.

For the second position, where 33 is residing, we start scanning the rest of the list in a linear manner.

We find that 14 is the second lowest value in the list and it should appear at the second place. We swap these values.

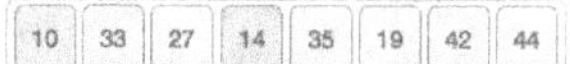

After two iterations, two least values are positioned at the beginning in a sorted manner.

The same process is applied to the rest of the items in the array.

Following is a pictorial depiction of the entire sorting process.

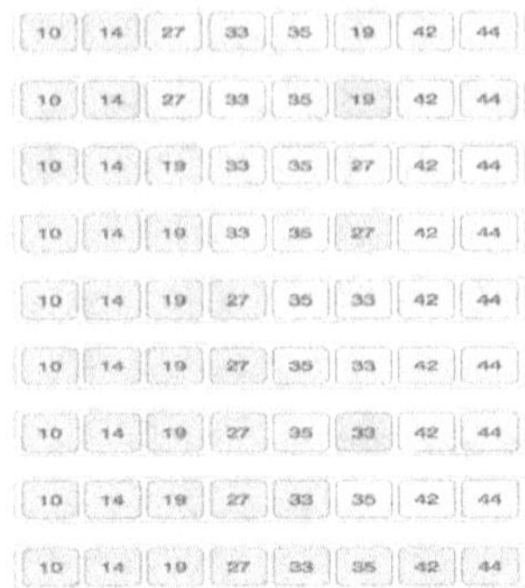

## Example 2

| Original Array | After 1st pass | After 2nd pass | After 3rd pass | After 4th pass | After 5th pass |
|---|---|---|---|---|---|
| 3 | 1 | 1 | 1 | 1 | 1 |
| 6 | 6 | 3 | 3 | 3 | 3 |
| 1 | 3 | 6 | 4 | 4 | 4 |
| 8 | 8 | 8 | 8 | 5 | 5 |
| 4 | 4 | 4 | 6 | 6 | 6 |
| 5 | 5 | 5 | 5 | 8 | 8 |

In the first pass, the smallest element found is 1, so it is placed at the first position, then leaving first element, smallest element is searched from the rest of the elements, 3 is the smallest, so it is then placed at the second position. Then we leave 1 and 3, from the rest of the elements, we search for the smallest and put it at third position and keep doing this, until array is sorted.

## Example 3

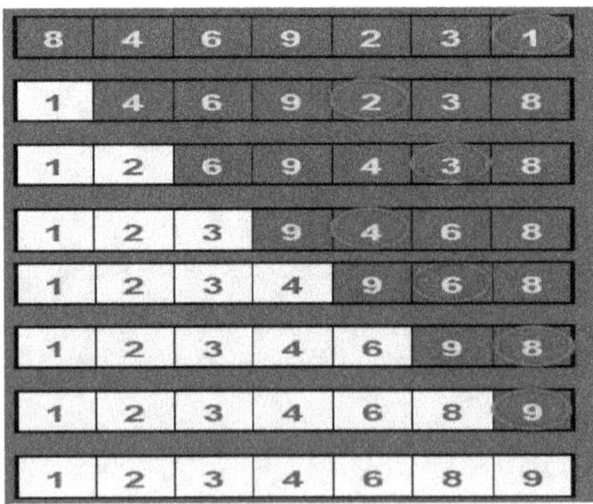

## Program

```c
#include<stdio.h>
int main(){
 int s,i,j,temp,a[20];
 printf("Enter total elements: ");
 scanf("%d",&s);
 printf("Enter %d elements: ",s);
 for(i=0;i<s;i++)
   scanf("%d",&a[i]);
 for(i=0;i<s;i++){
   for(j=i+1;j<s;j++){
     if(a[i]>a[j]){
       temp=a[i];
       a[i]=a[j];
       a[j]=temp;
     }
   }
 }
 printf("After sorting is: ");
 for(i=0;i<s;i++)
   printf(" %d",a[i]);
 return 0;
}
```

━━━━━━━━━ **CHAPTER 9** ━━━━━━━━━

# EXTERNAL SORTING

It is used for sorting when the data to be sorted is too large to fit into primary memory.

## 9.1. The Simple Algorithm (2-way merge)

Let us consider 4 tapes Ta1,Ta2,Tb1,Tb2. Let the size of the run(M) is 3

| Ta1 | 44 80 12 35 45 58 75 60 24 48 92 98 85 |
|-----|------|
| Ta2 | |
| Tb1 | |
| Tb2 | |

Initial Run Construction:

Step 1: Read M records at a time from the input tape Ta1.

Step 2: Sort the records internally and write the resultant records alternately to Tb1 and Tb2.

| Ta1 | | | |
|-----|------|------|------|
| Ta2 | | | |
| Tb1 | 12 44 80 | 24 60 75 | 85 |
| Tb2 | 35 45 58 | 48 92 98 | |

First Pass:

| Ta1 | 12 35 44 45 58 80 | 85 |
|-----|------|------|
| Ta2 | 24 48 60 75 92 98 | |
| Tb1 | | |
| Tb2 | | |

Second Pass:

| Ta1 | |
|-----|------|
| Ta2 | |
| Tb1 | 12 24 35 44 45 48 58 60 75 80 92 98 |
| Tb2 | 85 |

Third Pass:

| Ta1 | 12 24 35 44 45 48 58 60 75 80 85 92 98 |
|-----|------|
| Ta2 | |
| Tb1 | |
| Tb2 | |

It requires log(N/M) passes = log(13/3)=3

## 9.2.    Multiway Merge: [K way]

The number of passes required to sort an input can be reduced by increasing the number of tapes.

| | | |
|---|---|---|
| Ta1 | | |
| Ta2 | | |
| Ta3 | | |
| Tb1 | 12  44  80 | 48  92  98 |
| Tb2 | 35  45  58 | 85 |
| Tb3 | 24  60  75 | |

First Pass:

| | |
|---|---|
| Ta1 | 12  24  35  44  45  58  60  75  80 |
| Ta2 | 48  85  92  98 |
| Ta3 | |
| Tb1 | |
| Tb2 | |
| Tb3 | |

Second Pass:

| | |
|---|---|
| Ta1 | |
| Ta2 | |
| Ta3 | |
| Tb1 | 12  24  35  44  45  48  58  60  75  80  85  92  98 |
| Tb2 | |
| Tb3 | |

It requires $\log_k(N/M)$ passes

## 9.3.    Polyphase Merge

Let us consider 3 tapes T1,T2,T3 and an input file on T1 and produce 8 runs.

Equal distribution      - 4+4

Unequal distribution  - 7+1

Fibonacci distribution – 3+5

| Tapes | Run | After T2+T3 | After T1+T2 | After T2+T3 | After T1+T2 | After T2+T3 | After T1+T2 | After T2+T3 |
|---|---|---|---|---|---|---|---|---|
| T1 | 0 | 1 | 0 | 1 | 0 | 1 | 0 | 1 |
| T2 | 7 | 6 | 5 | 4 | 3 | 2 | 1 | 0 |
| T3 | 1 | 0 | 1 | 0 | 1 | 0 | 1 | 0 |

## 9.4.  Replacement Selection

M records are read into memory and placed in a priority queue.

Example 1: 5  2  9  7  0  8  1  6  3  4

Consider M=3   (*- dead cells)

Run 1

| Register | output | |
|---|---|---|
| 5  2  9 | 2 | Insert 7 |
| 5  7  9 | 5 | Insert 0 (0<5) |
| 0* 7  9 | 7 | Insert 8 |
| 0* 8  9 | 8 | Insert 1 (1<8) |
| 0* 1* 9 | 9 | Insert 6 |
| 0* 1* 6* | | |

Run 2

| Register | output | |
|---|---|---|
| 0  1  6 | 0 | Insert 3 |
| 3  1  6 | 1 | Insert 4 |
| 3  4  6 | 3 | |
| 4  6 | 4 | |
| 6 | 6 | |

Example 2: 44  80  12  35  45  58  75  60  24  48  92  98  85

Run 1

| Register | output | |
|---|---|---|
| 44  80  12 | 12 | Insert 35 |
| 44  80  35 | 35 | Insert 45 |
| 44  80  45 | 44 | Insert 58 |
| 58  80  45 | 45 | Insert 75 |
| 58  80  75 | 58 | Insert 60 |
| 60  80  75 | 60 | Insert 24 |
| 24* 80 75 | 75 | Insert 48 |
| 24* 80 48* | 80 | Insert 92 |
| 24* 92 48* | 92 | Insert 98 |
| 24* 98 48* | 98 | Insert 85 |
| 24* 85* 48* | | |

**Run 2**

| Register | output | |
|---|---|---|
| 24  85  48 | 48 | Insert 24 |
| 85  48 | 48 | Insert 48 |
| 85 | 85 | Insert 85 |

# CHAPTER 10

# SEARCHING ALGORITHM

Searching is a method to search a data item in the given set. There are two types of searching. They are

a.  Linear Search

b.  Binary Search

## 10.1.  Linear Search: (Sequential Search)

A linear search is the basic and simple search algorithm. A linear search searches an element or value from an array till the desired element or value is not found and it searches in a sequence order. It compares the element with all the other elements given in the list and if the element is matched it returns the value index else it returns -1. Linear Search is applied on the unsorted or unordered list when there are fewer elements in a list.

### *Routine for Linear Search*

```
function findIndex(values, target)
{
  for(var i = 0; i < values.length; ++i)
   {
    if (values[i] == target)
     {
       return i;
     }
   }
   return -1;
}
//call the function findIndex with array and number to be searchedfindIndex([ 8 , 2 , 6 , 3 , 5 ] , 5 ) ;
```

### *Analysis of Linear Search*

Best Case Analysis: O(1)

Average Case Analysis: O(N)

Worst Case Analysis: O(N)

## 10.2. Binary Search

Binary Search is applied on the sorted array or list. In binary search, we first compare the value with the elements in the middle position of the array. If the value is matched, then we return the value. If the value is less than the middle element, then it must lie in the lower half of the array and if it's greater than the element then it must lie in the upper half of the array. We repeat this procedure on the lower (or upper) half of the array. Binary Search is useful when there are large numbers of elements in an array.

### *Example*

For a binary search to work, it is mandatory for the target array to be sorted. We shall learn the process of binary search with a pictorial example. The following is our sorted array and let us assume that we need to search the location of value 31 using binary search.

First, we shall determine half of the array by using this formula

mid = low + (high - low) / 2

Here it is, 0 + (9 - 0 ) / 2 = 4 (integer value of 4.5). So, 4 is the mid of the array.

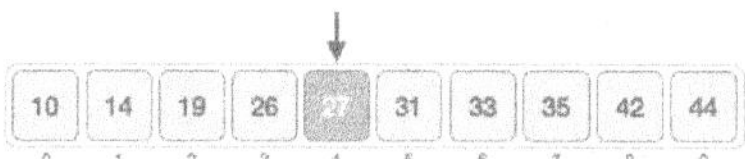

Now we compare the value stored at location 4, with the value being searched, i.e. 31. We find that the value at location 4 is 27, which is not a match. As the value is greater than 27 and we have a sorted array, so we also know that the target value must be in the upper portion of the array.

We change our low to mid + 1 and find the new mid value again.

low = mid + 1

mid = low + (high - low) / 2

Our new mid is 7 now. We compare the value stored at location 7 with our target value 31.

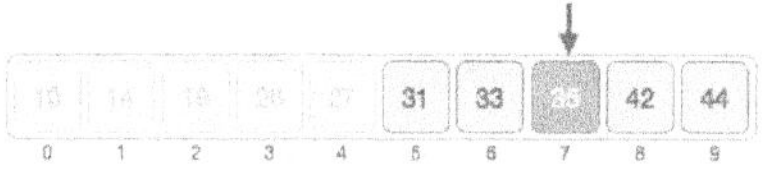

The value stored at location 7 is not a match, rather it is less than what we are looking for. So, the value must be in the lower part from this location.

Hence, we calculate the mid again. This time it is 5.

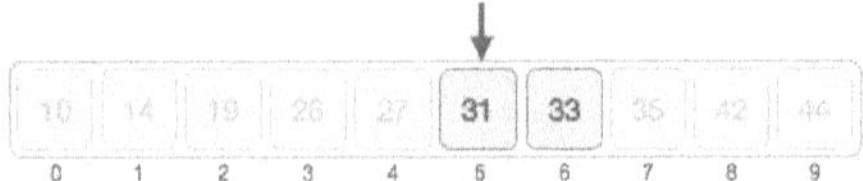

We compare the value stored at location 5 with our target value. We find that it is a match.

We conclude that the target value 31 is stored at location 5.

Binary search halves the searchable items and thus reduces the count of comparisons to be made to very less numbers.

### *Routine for Binary Search*

```
void Binary_Search(int X,int a[],int n)
{
int lower,upper,mid;
lower=1;
upper=n;
while(lower<upper)
{
mid=(lower+upper)/2;
if(X>a[mid])
lower=mid+1;
else if(X>a[mid])
upper=mid-1;
else
{
printf("Element found");
break;
}}
}
```

### *Analysis of Binary Search*

Best Case Analysis      : O(1)
Average Case Analysis : O(log N)
Worst Case Analysis    : O(log N)

# APPENDIX

## References


1. Mark. Allen. Weiss, "Data Structures and Algorithm Analysis in C", Fourth Edition, Pearson Education Asia, 2013

2. Y. Langsam, M. J. Augenstein and A. M. Tenenbaum, "Data Structures using C and C++", Second Edition, Prentice-Hall of India, 2009.

3. Alfred V. Aho, John E. Hopcroft and Jeffry D. Ullman, "Data Structures & Algorithms", Pearson Education, New Delhi, 2009.